The Christian as Minister

An Inquiry into Ordained Ministry,
Commissioned Ministries,
and Church Certification in
The United Methodist Church

Fourth Edition
1997
Robert F. Kohler and Joaquín García, editors

Editorial Committee
Theodore Hepner
Delano M. McIntosh
Timothy E. Moss
Rena Yocom

Unless otherwise noted, Scripture quotations are from the New Revised Standard Version Bible. Copyright © 1989 by the Division of Christian Education of the National Council of the Churches of Christ in the USA. Used by permission.

Disciplinary quotations are from *The Book of Discipline of The United Methodist Church – 1996*. Copyright © 1996 by The United Methodist Publishing House and from *The Book of Discipline of The United Methodist Church – 1992*. Copyright © 1992 by The United Methodist Publishing House. Used by permission.

Quotations are taken from *The United Methodist Book of Worship*. Copyright © 1992 by The United Methodist Publishing House. Used by permission.

Printed in the United States of America.

ISBN 0-938162-13-6

Cover design by Bret D. Haines

Photography credits: Boston University School of Theology Photo Services, pages 4, 28; Steve Shafer/General Board of Global Ministries, page 8; United Methodist Communications, pages 10, 52; Jack Corn, page 12; Mike DuBose/United Methodist Communications, pages 17, 33; John C. Goodwin/General Board of Global Ministries, pages 18, 98; Bret Haines/General Board of Higher Education and Ministry, page 24; American University, page 36; John Harnish/General Board of Higher Education and Ministry, page 49; Illinois Great Rivers Conference, page 57; K Karpen, page 58; Amanda Wells/General Board of Global Ministries, pages 60, 62; Jeneane Jones/General Board of Global Ministries, pages 71, 88; Kathy Gilbert/General Board of Higher Education and Ministry, page 73; General Board of Global Ministries, page 84; Kolya Braun/General Board of Global Ministries, page 86; Methodist Theological School in Ohio, page 90; United Theological Seminary, page 92; Drew University, The Theological School, page 102.

The Christian as Minister

This resource is a compilation of information about the call to ministry and the avenues The United Methodist Church offers to embody that call. It is based in the concept of servant ministry and servant leadership presented by the Council of Bishops and affirmed by the 1996 General Conference in ¶115 of *The Book of Discipline*.

Contents

The Spirit of the Lord is upon me because He hath anointed Me to preach

Introduction

The Christian as Minister is an introduction to ministry in The United Methodist Church. It contains an overview of the nature and mission of the church, the meaning of baptism, and the call to servant leadership as well as a description of the basic forms through which ministry is expressed in the connectional structure. The process through which church members enter lay ministry, diaconal ministry, ordained ministry (deacon or elder), chaplaincy, mission service, and licensed and certified ministries are conveniently outlined in this text.

The Christian as Minister is designed to be used as a part of the *Ministry Inquiry Process*, a vocational exploration program available to Christians interested in examining their relationship with God and asking the question: What is it that God is calling me to do? The *Ministry Inquiry Process* offers opportunities for spiritual discernment in which a seeker and companion endeavor to follow God's leading in a shared spiritual journey. The focus is on a free and open exploration of one's sense of God's calling with the support of the church and the Christian companion. In this process, the companion serves as a guide and friend to the seeker. The only qualification required to be a seeker is the desire to examine one's life situation in relation to God's call to serve the needs of the world as God's creation.

The Christian as Minister and the guidebook for the *Ministry Inquiry Process* are available through Cokesbury bookstores and may be used with a companion trained in the conference, district, or local church to guide a seeker through this initial vocational journey. While this may be the primary setting in which the texts are designed to be used, there are many other settings where *The Christian as Minister* and the *Ministry Inquiry Process* may be useful:

- High school, college, young adult, and adult groups could be guided through a vocational exploration process in Sunday, weekend, or retreat settings.
- College and university students may wish to explore the meaning of Christian vocation with a campus minister or a group of college students.
- Couples could read together and discuss what they learn from the *Ministry Inquiry Process* and *The Christian as Minister*, since career and family decisions are often closely interrelated.
- Committees on Pastor/Staff Parish Relations and other local church groups may wish to read these texts in order to understand the meaning of and options for ministry in The United Methodist Church.

The "Guidelines for the Minister" and "Guidelines for the Pastor/Staff Parish Relations Committee" contained in *The Christian as Minister* may be particularly helpful in understanding how to give proper support and guidance to candidates for ordained ministry.

Acknowledgments

The fourth edition of *The Christian as Minister* attempts to explore the options for ministerial service in The United Methodist Church. Attention is given to lay service, diaconal ministry, ordained ministry (deacon and elder), chaplaincy and campus ministry, licensed and certified ministries, and mission service.

Robert Kohler has coordinated the revision of *The Christian as Minister* through the staff of the General Board of Higher Education and Ministry. We are grateful to the office of Laity in Ministry of the General Board of Discipleship, the office of Mission Personnel Resources of the General Board of Global Ministries, and the divisional representatives of the General Board of Higher Education and Ministry for their careful writing, review, and preparation of the text: Timothy E. Moss, Laity in Ministry; Rena Yocom, Mission Personnel Resources; Joaquín García, Section of Deacons and Diaconal Ministries; Delano M. McIntosh, Division of Higher Education; Theodore Hepner, Section of Chaplains and Related Ministries.

Our thanks are due also to the Office of Interpretation, specifically Terri Hiers, Kathy Gilbert, and Judy Smith for their editorial assistance, and Bret Haines for the layout and cover design; and to Richard A. Hunt, author of the first edition. Many of his thoughts and ideas were retained in this revision.

Chapter 1
The Christian as Servant Leader

The Nature and Mission of the Church

Moving into the twenty-first century tends to make us more aware of life around us and our part in it. We are more aware of the changes and economic, social, and political forces that contribute to the complexity of our society. This complex diversity is a reality in our lives, and we must learn to speak about it through the lens of our faith. The church is the community where we experience a relationship with God and define our beliefs. As a faith community, the church is not merely a human institution but the creative work of the Spirit of God. The church is a way to relate to God.

The church is defined as the community of faith, hope, and love. It is a sign of the Kingdom of God. *The Book of Discipline* defines the church as the people of God and heirs of God's covenant and promises as we find them in the Old and New Testaments. Covenant is understood as the unilateral initiative of God to offer grace to humankind, and the response of the people of God to live in faithful obedience to God's will.

In Abraham and Sarah we see an expression of this covenant that symbolizes the spiritual relationship between the chosen people and God. In Jesus Christ, we see the symbol of a new covenant, where God's grace and promise are bestowed upon all humankind.

> ¶101. *From the beginning, God has dealt with the human family through covenants: with Adam and Eve, Noah, Abraham, Sarah and Hagar, Moses; with Deborah, Ruth, and Jeremiah and other prophets. In each covenant, God offered the chosen people the blessings of providence and commanded of them obedience to the divine will and way, that through them all the world should be blessed (Genesis 18:18; 22:18). In the new covenant in Christ, yet another community of hope was called out and gathered up, with the same promise and condition renewed that all who believe and obey shall be saved and made ministers of Christ's righteousness. Our spiritual forebears stressed this biblical theme of covenant-making and covenant-keeping as central in Christian experience.*

> ¶102. *The biblical story is marred by disregarded covenants and disrupted moral order, by sin and rebellion, with the resulting tragedies of alienation, oppression, and disorder. In the gospel of the new covenant, God in Christ has provided a new basis for reconciliation: justification by faith and birth into a new life in the Spirit. This gift, marked by growth toward wholeness of life, is revealed in Christ who came not to be served but to serve (Mark 10:45) and to give his life for the world. Christ freely took the nature of a servant, carrying this servanthood to its utmost limits (Philippians 2:7).*

The church is a divine gift when coupled with human activity. We cannot separate the church from the community. The church is a faith community that transforms and liberates persons and institutions from personal and social forms of sin. Freedom and transformation are the critical work of the church in our time.

The church is both the body of Christ and participant in Christ's ministry. As a faith community the church is a sign that points to God's grace and love for all creation. It continues the work of God's creation in the world and in Jesus Christ. The church, in the midst of community

beset by brokenness, offers a vision of peace, wholeness, and unity which God wills for all creation.

The church's mission is to fulfill God's plan and action for reclaiming and restoring the relationship between God's humanity and all creation. It is this mission that gives the church's vision focus and drive, and which invigorates and guides the church. At the same time, mission is the response of the community of faith to what God has done and continues to do to restore and reclaim creation.

The church needs a clear understanding of its mission in order to continue facing new challenges where political power is used to dominate and blur the spiritual vision, where violence is sought as an answer to the problems in our society, and where the poor and oppressed are excluded and alienated.

Reflection: How have you experienced the church?

- In what ways have you experienced the church as a faith community?
- In what ways have you experienced the church as a response to what God has done and continues to do for humankind?
- For all creation?

Baptism

In The United Methodist Church, we believe there are two sacraments ordained by Christ—baptism and the Lord's Supper. We believe these two sacraments are outward and visible signs of God's love toward us. They are means of grace by which the Holy Spirit works invisibly in us quickening, strengthening, and confirming our faith in God.

We believe children, like adults, have a place among the people of God and are to be afforded the same holy privileges regardless of their age. When baptized as infants, they are to be nurtured in the faith and led to personal acceptance of Christ. Upon profession of their faith in Christ, they confirm their baptism.

The Baptismal Covenant carries the following welcome:

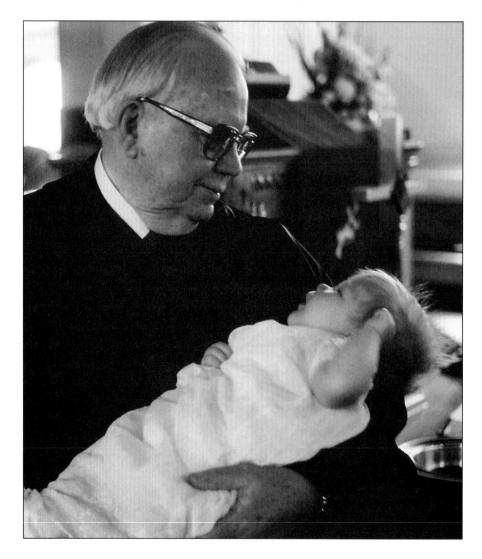

Through baptism
you are incorporated by the Holy Spirit
  into God's new creation
and made to share in Christ's royal priesthood.
We are all one in Christ Jesus.
With joy and thanksgiving we welcome you
  as members *of the family of Christ.*
                            —*The United Methodist Book of Worship*

This important aspect of the liturgy of the church serves to remind us that our lives on this earth are to be visible extensions of the life and ministry of Jesus. We are the hands, the feet, the arms, the legs, the mind, the heart—the manifestation of Christ in this world.

The Gospel chronicles Jesus starting his earthly ministry after his baptism by John the Baptist.

And when Jesus had been baptized, just as he came up from the water, suddenly the heavens were opened to him and he saw the Spirit of God descending like a dove and alighting on him. And a voice from heaven said, "This is my Son, the Beloved, with whom I am well pleased."

                            —Matthew 3:16-17

The baptism of Jesus Christ was a significant act, for it embodied God's blessing and anointing. It was a commissioning — an empowering grace through the work of the Holy Spirit. So by virtue of our baptism into the body of Christ, the church, we too are commissioned, anointed, and empowered to carry out the ministry that Jesus started when he walked this earth. That makes all baptized persons ministers.

Each of us is a minister to the world in Christ's name, whether our work involves people or things, whether we work alone or with others, whether we work for money or as a volunteer, whether our work binds up the world's hurts or calls the world to new hope and vision. Any work that binds up the world's hurts or calls the world to new hope and vision, any work done in Christ's name on Christ's behalf, is a witness to Christ's continuing presence in the world.

That Christ calls us all to witness and service cannot be denied. However, the kind of witness and the kind of service to which God is calling us is a far more difficult question to answer. This is the question of

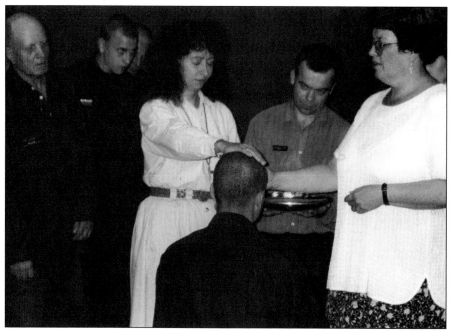

vocation, the place where God's will for our lives and our radical obedience meet in the fulfillment of our purpose for being.

If you are wrestling with the question of where God is calling you to live out the gospel, some of your anxiety may be addressed by looking carefully at the record of Jesus' struggle with his vocation and calling. There was a time in his life when Jesus did not know that he was to bear the history of God in a special way, a time when his vocation in life was not clearly understood. He struggled with who he was in relationship to God, and what it was that God intended for him to do. The agent of that discovery process was the Holy Spirit which, in his baptism, revealed him to be the beloved Son of God and led him into the wilderness to struggle with what identity with God meant in the work he would do.

Reflection

Even after Jesus had clarified his calling by making the vocational choices which allowed him to participate in God's story, that calling was not always affirmed by the people of God. Listen to this account of his ministry in the synagogue at Nazareth. Again, to which elements in this event can you relate?

> *When he came to Nazareth, where he had been brought up, he*
> *went to the synagogue on the sabbath day, as was his custom.*
> *He stood up to read, and the scroll of the prophet Isaiah was*

given to him. He unrolled the scroll and found the place where
it was written: "The Spirit of the Lord is upon me, because he
has anointed me to bring good news to the poor. He has sent
me to proclaim release to the captives and recovery of sight to
the blind, to let the oppressed go free, to proclaim the year of
the Lord's favor." And he rolled up the scroll, gave it back to
the attendant, and sat down. The eyes of all in the synagogue
were fixed on him. Then he began to say to them, "Today this
scripture has been fulfilled in your hearing." All spoke well of
him and were amazed at the gracious words that came from his
mouth. They said, "Is not this Joseph's son?" He said to them,
"Doubtless you will quote to me this proverb, 'Doctor, cure
yourself!' And you will say, 'Do here also in your hometown
the things that we have heard you did at Capernaum.'" And he
said, "Truly I tell you, no prophet is accepted in the prophet's
hometown. . . ." When they heard this, all in the synagogue
were filled with rage. They got up, drove him out of the town,
and led him to the brow of the hill on which their town was
built, so that they might hurl him off the cliff. But he passed
through the midst of them and went on his way.
—Luke 4:16-24; 28-30

The vocation of Jesus Christ was and is radically different than your vocation; nevertheless, there is a relationship between his vocation and yours. It is not accidental that you can identify with elements in Jesus' baptism, wilderness journey, and ministry. His struggle with vocational choice was as real as yours. In a way, your vocation in life grows out of his because, through the Holy Spirit, Christ is inviting you to share in God's story by witnessing to its reality in your life and living it out through your actions. Like Christ and the Apostles and the host of saints who have gone before you in the faith, you are called to discover the meaning of your vocation in the story living and story telling of the gospel. While the ways in which you tell it and the service you render in obedience to the will of God will differ from all others who surround you in the faith, you will find in that vocation, and only there, a true sense of who you are in relationship to God and who it is that you were meant to become.

As a Christian, you are called to be a minister of Christ. In yourself this is an impossible task, but in the power of the Holy Spirit all things are possible. The only questions that remain are: To what kind of ministry is God calling you that will meet your deepest need and the world's deepest hunger? What work would God have you do in the name of Christ, for the sake of the world?

Reflection

Bill McElvaney is someone who struggles with living out his vocation —no matter what it might be—as a Christian. A former administrator in a seminary, Bill tells this story about a worship experience that refocused his thinking about what he did day in and day out:

> *At Saint Paul School of Theology we have chapel services on Tuesday and Thursday mornings. Often these are rich experiences of worship. For me a recent Eucharist service turned into a feast of hearing and receiving in a totally unexpected manner. . . . On this occasion . . . a deeper vision of what it means to be an . . . administrator came to me as I was sitting in the pew looking at the elements on the communion table. . . .*
>
> *I began to realize that I was being asked the question, "What does it mean for the desk in my office to become that communion table?" I began to see one superimposed on the other, so that the elements rested on the united form of the two. The loaf and the chalice touched everything on my desk and all the transactions that came across it. I knew that sitting behind a Eucharistic desk, I would never administer the seminary in quite the same way as before. I knew that every administrative detail and decision would in some way represent the hurts and the hopes of human beings, that the brokenness and wholeness of life would be at stake on this desk become table, that even roof repairs and HEW forms would point beyond themselves to the total task of the Risen Lord and the Easter People.*
>
> —William K. McElvaney, *The People of God in Ministry*
> (Nashville: Abingdon Press,1981), 116-17.

Servant Leadership

The Call to Servant Leadership

Few people today automatically enter the same occupation as their parents. Some just drift into an occupation or follow the advice or pressure of parents or teachers or friends. The more deliberate may choose an occupation for themselves by considering what they do best or what they most enjoy doing, or if they are systematic, by considering the pros and cons of various trades or professions and by studying job listings.

Another way to look at this is to say that a person may become an accountant or a plumber or a physician either by default, as a result of social pressure, or by a deliberate and careful choice.

A call to a particular vocation is a fourth category. Though a call might have elements of any of the preceding categories, a call is something above and beyond all of them. A call is not something a person does by default or under social pressure or entirely by free choice. For a call implies a caller. And the Caller, in the case of those summoned to ministry, is outside the immediate social world. The Caller is God.

The concept of call has been applied to three distinct experiences. These experiences are loosely linked to the three persons of the Trinity:

1. God the Creator calls people into being. The word *call* here is used in rather a loose sense, but it does refer to an important dimension of our relationship to God—a dimension that we share with all of humanity.

2. God the Redeemer calls persons to accept God's grace. This call is manifested in the Christian community, and persons respond to this call by a commitment to the Christian community. This is what binds us with all other Christians in the ministry of all believers.

3. God the Spirit calls some persons to a public form of servant leadership within the church. Empowered and guided by the Holy Spirit, individuals respond to that call with a life-changing and lifelong commitment to service

For a further exploration of your call to servant ministry, talk with your pastor or another United Methodist minister about the Ministry Inquiry Process.

What It Means to be a Servant Leader

God calls people to be in ministry. The Bible has many accounts of God's call to very different individuals: to Amos, to Moses, to Jeremiah, to Paul. God calls such people to become servants and leaders. But this call to become servants and leaders is not a call to two separate categories or tasks or functions. Instead, it is a call to one role — the role of servant leader.

In order to explore the role of the servant leader, consider these two points:

1. Servant leadership is a paradox, an apparent contradiction in terms. But while servant leadership is a paradox, it is not a contradiction. That is, servant and leader are not opposite terms. The opposite of a leader is a follower. Leaders and followers are mutually exclusive; a person cannot at the same time lead people and follow those same people.

   On the other hand, the opposite of a servant is a master. A person cannot at the same time both serve a group of people and be their master.

   The word *servant* does not mean follower; the word *leader* does not mean master. This discussion is not about followers or masters but about service and leadership. The same person can be both servant and leader.

2. In most societies, including present day American society, many people are socialized or programmed, as it were, to become either servants or leaders. Through cultural conditioning or through the operation of social structures some of us may be more predisposed to leadership roles, others to servant roles. Historically such a division has often been made on the basis of gender or ethnic group. In order to become a servant leader, a person must recognize her or his own predisposition. Those who see themselves as servants will need to learn to exercise leadership because in God's realm the effective servant becomes a leader. Those who see themselves as leaders need to learn to serve, because in God's realm the real leaders are those who serve most effectively.[1]

Identifying Marks of Servant Leaders

In the book, *Contemporary Images of Christian Ministry*,[2] Don Messer identifies four marks for servant leaders today.

1. *Servant leaders understand ministry as basically not a status but a service to humanity.* They are not elevated to status offices but called to specialized positions to expend themselves for others. Jesus said, "whoever wishes to become great among you must be your servant, and whoever wishes to be first among you must be slave of all. For the Son of Man came not to be served but to serve, and to give his life a ransom for many." (Mark 10:43b-45)

2. *Servant leaders recognize that authority is fundamentally not ascribed by position but derived from service.* Power is not given

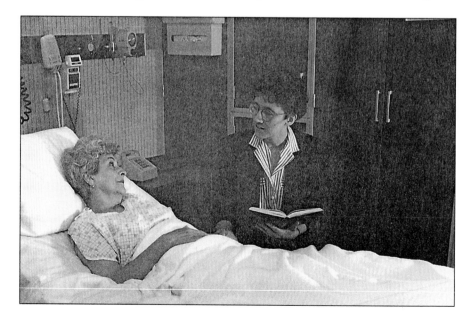

automatically by employment, election, or appointment; it is more often gained by loving service. Even in the rough and tumble world of partisan politics, there are those who understand power as servanthood. Former President Jimmy Carter once remarked that he should not be viewed as "First Boss" but as "First Servant." Senator Mark O. Hatfield stated that the Christian in politics "is called to be a servant-leader. Self preservation is no longer the key motive of all political activities; rather, it becomes the service of human need, and prophetic faithfulness to a vision of God's will being done 'on earth as it is in heaven.'"[3]

3. *Servant leaders are empathetic to the human condition, understanding all life to be ambiguous and truth often paradoxical.* To be a Christian means having a tolerance for imperfection. The enigma of human nature, Robert Greenleaf has noted, is that even the typically imperfect person can be:

    > *capable of great dedication and heroism if wisely led. Many otherwise able people are disqualified to lead because they cannot work with and through the half-people who are all there are. The secret of institution building is to be able to weld a team of such people by lifting them up to grow taller than they would otherwise be.*[4]

4. *Servant leaders are pathfinders and not simply problem solvers.* Pathfinders are problem solvers, able to sort through confusing issues, organize responses, and resolve differences. But pathfinders are more than mundane problem solvers. They have a vision of what the future should look like, how persons need to be motivated and organizations changed, and what values need to triumph. Pathfinders are not just facilitating conflict managers, but persons of passionate Christian commitment with a gift for inspiring others to work together toward achieving those commitments.

Reflection

Jesus, knowing that the Father had given all things into his hands, and that he had come from God and was going to God, got up from the table, took off his outer robe, and tied a towel around himself. Then he poured water into a basin and began to wash the disciples' feet and to wipe them with the towel.

—John 13:3-5

Ask yourself in what ways do you feel God is calling you to be a servant leader? Think of the ways you can lead people in the community or in your peer group to serve the needs that surround you.

Notes

1. From Simon Parker, *The Call to Servant Leadership* (Nashville: Division of Diaconal Ministry, General Board of Higher Education and Ministry, The United Methodist Church), 1989.

2. Donald E. Messer, *Contemporary Images of Christian Ministry* (Nashville: Abingdon Press, 1989), 106-112.

3. Mark O. Hatfield, *Between a Rock and a Hard Place* (Dallas: Word Inc., 1976), 27.

4. Robert Greenleaf, *Servant Leadership*, (New York: Paulist Press, 1977), 20.

Chapter 2
Images of Servant Leadership

The Connectional Structure

Now there are varieties of gifts, but the same Spirit; and there are varieties of services, but the same Lord; and there are varieties of activities, but it is the same God who activates all of them in everyone.

—1 Corinthians 12:4-6

The gifts he gave were that some would be apostles, some prophets, some evangelists, some pastors and teachers, to equip the saints for the work of ministry, for building up the body of Christ.

—Ephesians 4:11-12

There are varieties of gifts and varieties of ministry for those who would be servant leaders in The United Methodist Church, and all are called to equip the saints for the work of ministry and build up the body of Christ. In order to help you explore these options and clarify what it is that you need to do most in life, a number of settings for laity, diaconal ministers, permanent deacons, elders, and the mission personnel of the General Board of Global Ministries are described in the following chapters.

The primary setting for all forms of ministry in The United Methodist Church is its connectional structure. For John Wesley, that structure was not a hierarchy of interrelated conferences, boards, and agencies, but a loosely knit structure in which Christians of like mind and like spirit linked arms in common cause. "If thine heart is as my heart . . . give me thine hand," said Wesley.

Today connectionalism in the United Methodist tradition is multi-levelled, global in nature, and local in thrust.

For us connectionalism is not merely a linking of one connectional charge conference to another horizontally across the globe. It is rather a vital web of interactive and intertwining relationships that enable us to

express freely, justly, and in dignity at both global and local levels our essential identity, inclusive fellowship, common mission, distinctive ethos, and visible unity.

We are connected by sharing a common tradition of faith, including our Doctrinal Standards and General Rules (¶67); by sharing together a constitutional polity, including a leadership of general superintendency; by sharing a common mission which we seek to carry out together both globally and locally; by working together organizationally in and through conferences that reflect the inclusive and missional character of our fellowship; by sharing a common ethos which characterizes our distinctive way of doing things.

Excerpted from "The Study of the Ministry of The United Methodist Church" report to the 1996 General Conference, The Council of Bishops, The United Methodist Church.

The Ministry of the Laity

The person who receives his or her first call from God to be in ministry is always a layperson. That call may lead to ordination or consecration, but it won't start that way. When Jesus called his disciples or the apostle Paul he wasn't calling clergy. It is arguable that he would ever have called them clergy. But they were most assuredly called to ministry. "Go, therefore, and make disciples . . ." was a directive to all of the *laos*. God does call laypersons into ministry.

There are endless opportunities for ministry. They are all around us wherever we are, whatever we do. Most of these opportunities can be and are carried out by laypersons. There is a special credibility in being in ministry as a layperson simply because it is not something you have to be. Being a credible and respected layperson provides a tremendous opportunity for witness. Most of the time the layperson is a volunteer, carrying out a ministry because it is satisfying or there is a special joy in it. A person's job can be carried out as a ministry, almost without regard for what the job is. Ministry can be carried out at home, on the street, at play, at work, or wherever else one might find one's self. Of course, one's job just might be a ministry. Laypersons are also employed by local congregations or church agencies or work for charitable organizations in a wide variety of capacities.

It is important to remember that all persons are parts of the body of Christ. As Paul tells us in 1 Corinthians 12:4, "Now there are varieties of gifts, but the same Spirit. . . ." All are called to be ministers, but most are

not called to ordained or diaconal ministry. Very few ministries absolutely require clergy to carry them out, and there are many ministries that are best handled by laity. And there are enough laypersons within the body of Christ with the right spiritual gifts to handle the opportunities. What is important is that laypersons pray earnestly for guidance and discernment in identifying their individual gifts so that the needs are met.

Images of Servant Leadership

Joan is an accountant with a government agency. She is also the director of lay speaking ministries in her district. Sunday is an extremely busy day most weeks. Today she is filling the pulpit in a medium-sized church 20 miles from home. First service is at 8:00 a.m., and she will also preach at the 10:30 service. After the last service, she and her husband Bert—also a certified lay speaker—have a quick bite of lunch and head for the state penitentiary which is another 20-mile drive. Joan and Bert share a prison ministry with a group of members from their church. Every Sunday afternoon the group conducts a worship service for inmates followed by Bible study and then a group counseling and discussion session. This ministry is one in which Joan and Bert find great joy. It is growing and appreciated by inmates and prison authorities alike. Joan and Bert find themselves home, exhausted, at 8:00 p.m.

Jim is an electrical engineer and the plant manager for an automotive parts manufacturer. He loves and cares for the people in his charge. He mentors them and trusts them to do their jobs. Monday is extremely busy. It is the day when the previous week's activities are reviewed and the current week's plans are finalized, among other things. Breakfast with a coworker is the first order of the day. This person is having personal problems which are negatively affecting her job. Jim offers counsel and reassurance to her. The occasion offers Jim an opportunity to witness. Soon after arriving at the plant, there is a meeting with technical sales persons to review customer performance. This is followed by meetings with production schedulers and then cost accounting. At noon, Jim has a luncheon meeting with the other board members of an agency which trains and employs the handicapped. As a board member himself, he gives a great deal of time to agency management. He also hires agency clients whenever he can. In the afternoon, Jim walks the production lines, stopping frequently to listen to the concerns and ideas of workers. Finally, he meets with supervisors and a self-directed work team. After dinner with his family, he and his wife Marcia head to their church for Disciple Bible Study.

Marie is director of volunteers for a large suburban United Methodist church. She has several degrees and experience as a social worker. The position is paid and is the sole support for her and her two teenage children. Her work is generally with the Council on Ministries which she has helped transform from a dull, inward-focused body to a creative consultative group which constantly seeks new opportunities for ministry in the community. Her Tuesday started with a short updating of the pastor-in-charge on two or three major outreach activities. Then she went to a board meeting of the local Habitat for Humanity, an organization strongly supported by the church. From there she went to a luncheon meeting of the United Way board, of which she is a member. In the afternoon she met with two church members over a proposal for a new ministry which needed church support. Some quiet time was then spent in her office contemplating how to handle a program she felt no longer deserved support. Before dinner Marie prepared for a presentation to the finance committee which was to be held that evening.

Arnie is a retired journeyman carpenter and a widower. Arnie is a hospital visitor and also works with hospice. He has received extensive training in caregiving and has received a certification from local United Methodist hospitals as an associate chaplain. This gives him entree at most local hospitals and extended care facilities. His Wednesday starts at 8:00 a.m. on a Habitat for Humanity job site where he will supervise construction for a half day. In the afternoon he will make his hospital rounds, a task which he does three times per week. He does his hospice work on alternate afternoons and is always on call. Arnie works full time as a volunteer which satisfies him immensely. He misses his wife, but he is no longer lonely.

Marilyn and Bill have been married more than 20 years. Their oldest son recently died after a long, wasting illness. Their faith and the support of their congregation have helped them deal with their grief. While their son was ill, they developed the idea for a ministry to help grieving people cope with loss and grow from it. They were able to sell the idea to their church's administrative council, thereby getting a place from which to work and some seed money to start. They began with a hot line and ads in local papers and the yellow pages. They had recently started several support groups and saw the need for more. These have been opportunities for witness. Volunteers have been no problem, even coming from other churches. They have been successful at getting counseling professionals such as clergy, social workers, and psychologists to train volunteers gratis. The problems they are having come from too much success, too fast. They need to find a more permanent and considerably larger home and some permanent staff—and they have very little money. Marilyn has quit her job as a legal secretary to give full time to the ministry. Bill has to continue with his job at the paper mill to keep the family afloat, but he devotes all the time he can to the ministry. It is Thursday and both of them are meeting with a United Way committee to seek additional funding.

Nancy and Georgie are best of friends. They are middle-aged, single, working women. Georgie is a widow and Nancy a divorcee. Their children are all on their own. Through their churches, both have become involved with a Salvation Army shelter for the homeless. Through their growing interest in the shelter, they have taken on more and more responsibility and activity. Georgie is now director of volunteers, and Nancy is placement director, an office in charge of locating permanent residences and jobs for their clients. Three days each week they have arranged to be at the shelter at midday to help with cooking and serving meals. Fridays are one of their days. Both will be back in the late afternoon after work to put in several more hours at their desks. Then they will have a late dinner together and discuss their plans for the coming week.

Dick is a Certified Public Accountant and self-employed. Through his involvement with lay speaking ministry, he first became aware of a small, rural church some 20 miles from his home. He has now become a local pastor serving that church. He loves the job. He has also started with the Course of Study for his credentials. The church cannot support him, so he must also maintain his accounting practice in order to live. His wife and his children have been enthusiastic supporters and have really become part of the ministry to this church. The church is flourishing. Attendance is up, and there are actually some new members. It is Saturday and, except for emergencies, that is his only opportunity to visit people and to make hospital calls. That and putting the finishing touches on his sermon will occupy the entire day.

These vignettes give only a glimpse of the enormous variety of opportunity for ministry available to laypersons. The person seeking to identify his or her call should investigate the possibilities.

Reflection
- Did any of the vignettes interest you? Think about opportunities for service that have piqued your interest.
- Do you have gifts or interests that lend themselves to particular opportunities for ministry?
- Have you noticed opportunities for ministry related to your job?

Varieties of Diaconal Ministry

Among the people of God there are those whom God calls to specialized ministry. The options for vocational service as a diaconal minister in The United Methodist Church are many. As old as the New Testament, the office of diaconal minister in The United Methodist Church has its origin in the biblical and historical Christian heritage, in theological understandings of ministry, and in the outreach for the church both within and beyond the local congregation. As such, the office is an integral part of the total ministry of the church with membership in the annual conference. Diaconal ministry exists to intensify and make more effective the self-understanding of the whole people of God as servants in Christ's name. The purpose of diaconal ministry is the equipping of the general ministry of the church to the end that the whole church may be built up as the Body of Christ for the work of ministry.

> *The diaconal ministers are called to specialized ministries of service, justice, and love within local congregations and in the wider world. Servant ministry must always involve a concern for justice as well as a love for persons. Diaconal ministers focus their service through a variety of ministries, such as, administration, education, evangelism, music, health ministries, and community development—to the local congregation and the wider community.*

Christ's service to humankind and the Church's responsibility for continuing that service in the world are both symbolized and enabled especially, but not exclusively, in diaconal ministry. Diaconal ministry exists to intensify and make more effective the self-understanding of the whole people of God as servants in Christ's name.

—¶109, *1992 Discipline*

The United Methodist Church has recognized the importance of the ministry of service by establishing the office of diaconal minister in 1976. Diaconal ministers are members of The United Methodist Church who seek a more effective witness on behalf of the church in the communities or vocations where they serve.

The 1996 General Conference recognized that the call to a ministry of service may be expressed in the ministry of deacon. For this reason, no new candidates for diaconal ministry will be accepted after January 1, 1997. Those who are in candidacy prior to that date will be allowed to finish their candidacy requirements and be consecrated according to the *1992 Discipline*. Consecrated diaconal ministers may transfer to become ordained deacons in full connection according to the transitional provisions available until December 31, 2000.

Diaconal ministers are called to build up and equip the church for action in the world through education, evangelism, worship, music, and

counseling but also are involved in outreach through ministries to persons with disabilities through community and social service agencies, are involved in advocacy for the powerless, and work with government agencies, campus ministries, church communications and administration, teaching, counseling, drug rehabilitation, and more. Wherever the needs of the world are evidenced, the church is called to minister, and diaconal ministers may be called upon to serve.

Steve is the administrator of a United Methodist Home for children and youth. This institution serves those who suffer from neglect and physical and emotional abuse. The support and care that an ordained minister provided to Steve in his high school years made a great impact on his answering the call to diaconal ministry. He explains that his call to ministry is an incarnate expression of the scripture passage "And whoever gives even a cup of cold water to one of these little ones. . . ." (Matthew 10:42)

Denise is a graduate from a United Methodist theological seminary with a master's degree in Christian education. Her undergraduate degree from Illinois State University was in special education with the hearing impaired. Before becoming a diaconal minister, she taught in this area in the classroom for several years. Denise discerned that she had the gift of working with the hearing impaired and that her faith helped her to understand this as a gift from God for ministry. To quote Denise, "As Christ's servant, I am called to be an enabler of others in the world, facilitator of the work of the church, and a presenter of the ministry of Jesus Christ of love, justice, and service."

While working part time as a Christian educator in a United Methodist local church, Denise developed a proposal to organize a program to enable churches to explore new avenues of ministry. Ultimately the proposal calls for establishing or expanding their ministries to include hearing impaired persons and their families through identification, awareness, education, resources, support, and communication. She worked with a cluster of 20 congregations in the area to establish a directory

of hearing impaired persons living in their communities. Next she developed workshops and awareness programs to educate people about hearing impairment and the special needs of such people and their families.

Margaret is an associate executive director of church services in a United Methodist community center, which provides multiple services to persons from infancy to older adulthood. Margaret was planning to become a public school teacher until her senior year in college when she spent a summer working in the community center. That experience led her to a new sense of vocation. She became a diaconal minister as a response to her call to serve not only the African-American community, but also those in poverty.

A senior citizens project of a slightly different sort is housed at a United Methodist Church. The program includes telephone calls to elderly persons at night, a handyman repair service, an adult day-care program, and seminars on health issues, estate planning, and spiritual formation.

Ann graduated with a master's degree in Christian education. She has served as a missionary and presently is serving as director of adult ministries in the local church. Her functions as diaconal minister have been defined by the faith community to prepare, equip, and nurture the members of the community to witness and serve in the world.

Working in the area of Christian education, it is her purpose to help persons deepen their faith and become disciples in the marketplace. As a diaconal minister she participates in the liturgy of the church and helps to equip the church to address the needs of the community. She has developed such ministries as job match, career transition support group, divorce adjustment support seminars, a cancer support group, an Alzheimer's support group, single parent support groups helping single parents to be part of a faith community, grief seminars, a community referrals ministry, and ministries of the church for the homeless.

Social services plus a heavy emphasis on advocacy fill Ruth's days as coordinator of the community programs of United Ministries in a metropolitan area. It is a community ministry of three United Methodist churches. A recent emphasis was directed toward the local natural gas company trying to work out ways to prevent shutoff of heat during cold weather and to help the poor with better budgeting. A housing rehabilitation program has been in place for a year; work is done with neighborhood and support groups; and direct services focus on everything from summer camps and after-school programs to a youth drop-in center.

Jeff received his masters degree from a United Methodist theological seminary and is working as a diaconal minister of youth. His responsibilities vary from counseling youth and their parents about faith issues to education about drug and substance abuse prevention. He works with counselors and teachers and helps the church provide ways for youth to develop a mature faith. He meets with the youth in their schools and organizes events to deal with teenage pregnancy, suicide, depression, and vocations. These events are open to the community to serve beyond the walls of the building and help the youth to be involved in ministries of service through community projects.

As you can see, diaconal ministry is frequently a "hands on" ministry —a program of direct help where need is indicated. But it always has another focus—helping and equipping others in the church to fulfill their calls to service in the name of Christ.

Reflection: Gifts for diaconal ministry and needs of the world
- God calls people, not only for tasks in the church, but also for ministries in the world. Think about God's call in your life.
- Think about the gifts you have and see if you could use them in one of the diaconal settings mentioned above.
- What do you enjoy doing that might be related to diaconal ministry such as those cited above?
- Can you imagine yourself responding to the needs of your community or larger world through some of these diaconal forms of service?

The Ministry of the Deacon

From among the baptized, deacons are called by God to a lifetime of servant leadership, authorized by the Church, and ordained by a bishop. Deacons fulfill servant ministry in the world and lead the Church in relating the gathered life of Christians to their ministries in the world, interrelating worship in the gathered community with service to God in the world. Deacons give leadership in the Church's life: in the teaching and proclamation of the Word; in worship, and in assisting the elders in the administration of the sacraments of baptism and the Lord's Supper; in forming and nurturing disciples; in conducting marriages and burying the dead; in the congregation's mission to the world; and in leading the congregation in interpreting the needs, concerns, and hopes of the world. It is the deacons, in both person and function, whose distinctive ministry is to embody, articulate, and lead the whole people of God in its servant ministry.

From the earliest days of the church, deacons were called and set apart for the ministry of love, justice, and service; of connecting the church with the most needy, neglected, and marginalized among the children of God. This ministry grows out of the Wesleyan passion for social holiness and ministry among the poor.

Deacons lead the congregation in its servant ministry and equip and support all baptized Christians in their ministry. The distinct ministry of the deacon has evolved in United Methodism over many years – the continuing work of the deaconess, the home missionary, and the diaconal minister. The Church, recognizing the gifts and impact of all predecessor embodiments of the diaconate and providing for the continuation of the office of deaconess, affirms that this distinctiveness is made visible and central to the Church's life and ministry through ordination and that the ministry of the deacon is a faithful response of the mission of the Church meeting the emerging needs of the future. Deacons are accountable to the annual conference and the bishop for the fulfillment of their call to servant leadership.

Ministry, Authority, and Responsibilities of Deacons in Full Connection — 1. *Deacons are persons called by God, authorized by the Church, and ordained by a bishop to a lifetime ministry of Word and Service to both the community and the congregation in a ministry that connects the two. Deacons exemplify Christian discipleship and create opportunities for others to enter into discipleship. In the world, the deacon seeks to express a ministry of compassion and justice, assisting laypersons as they claim their own ministry. In the congregation, the ministry of the deacon is to teach and to form disciples, and to lead worship together with other ordained and laypersons.*

2. *The deacon in full connection shall have the rights of voice and vote in the annual conference where membership is held; shall be eligible to serve as clergy on boards, commissions, or committees of the annual conference and hold office on the same; and shall be eligible for election as a clergy delegate to General, central, or jurisdictional conference. The deacon in full connection shall attend all the sessions of the annual conference and share with elders in full connection responsibility for all matters of ordination, character, and conference relations of clergy (¶325.1). Any deacon in full connection unable to attend shall write the bishop requesting to be excused setting forth the reason for the absence.*

3. As members of the Order of Deacons, all deacons in full connection are in covenant with all other such deacons in the annual conference and shall participate in the life of their Order.

—¶¶319 and 320, *1996 Discipline*

Mary is a permanent ordained deacon who has combined her training as counselor with theological education to respond to her call to ministry. She serves as director of a crisis intervention center and believes that her work is an extension of the ministry of Jesus Christ and therefore of the church. In her office she deals with crisis phone calls from persons who are suffering with depression or persons who face problems in their lives and need to talk with someone who shows care and concern.

She is committed to connecting the needs of the community and the gifts and talents of the congregation where she is serving.

The area of health care is the setting for Naomi's ministry. She serves and fulfills her call as permanent ordained deacon as a parish nurse. At this time in history there are many older adults who need the services of a nurse. Naomi combines her licensed nursing skills with pastoral care and theological education to become a presence of the Body of Christ, the church, with the people.

Gene has responded to the call to be a permanent ordained deacon as a social worker with seminary training to serve as the director of a children's home which is a United Methodist agency. This agency has become a major provider of foster care for children who have been abandoned or physically or sexually abused. Gene notes that it is in the midst of suffering and oppression that the embodiment of the ministry of Jesus Christ needs to be present. He is connected with not one but all the churches in the area to interpret the tremendous need that exists in our society to give hope to our children. He incarnates the passage of Matthew 25:40 — "Truly I tell you, just as you did it to one of the least of these . . . you did it to me."

Martha is a professor in the community college, teaching multicultural studies. Her call as permanent ordained deacon is quite clear to her: "Faith has to be expressed in the marketplace. You need to have the support and authorization of the church to be involved in making a difference in this society. What I do as a teacher is not just a job or career but is a real call to bring reconciliation among people. The reason for me to teach here, is that we are all children of God, and we need to live in peace and harmony." She has a degree in multicultural studies with a seminary education.

Dean has been appointed as permanent ordained deacon to coordinate and mobilize a local church in outreach ministries. His ministry is to survey the needs within the community and determine how the congregation can be involved to respond to those needs. He has surveyed the congregation to determine the gifts, talents, and abilities of the congregation to make a significant presence and difference in the community, involving those church in the homeless program, hospice program, meals on wheels, respite care, Habitat for Humanity, prison ministries, halfway houses, shelter for battered women, and the care program for patients with AIDS. He sees the importance of the interrelatedness of the community and the congregation. His call to the diaconate is to bring into reality John Wesley's statement, "The world is my parish."

Kathy is a permanent ordained deacon in Christian education in the local church. She is quick to say that Christian education is theological education. It is more than Sunday school. It is also value and faith formation and should include everybody in the congregation. However, it is not ingrown but an outreach expression of our faith beliefs. Kathy said: "The church is the salt of our sanity. We are here to make a difference." She is excited about the commitment of the congregation to relate to the needs of society. The church has developed a program to adopt an inner city public elementary school to work with the children with remedial assistance, tutoring, enrichment programs, sports, and other extra curricular activities. However, that is not enough. They have a respite program for families with handicapping conditions.

The role of the permanent ordained deacon is as diverse as the needs in the world require. Sometimes the person feeling called to specialized ministry will work with the church structure or the structure of human service agencies to respond to the needs of the community. What is distinctive is that the person is committed to being accountable to the annual conference and the bishop, and to equipping him/herself to serve in a specialized area of ministry including theological education. No matter where they serve, the permanent ordained deacon will always be related to a local congregation helping them to also use their gifts in service to others.

Reflection

- Sandra Schneiders said that the scope of ministry is determined by the needs in our society; and to know the needs we need to prayerfully read the signs of the times. As you read the newspapers and watch and listen to the news, what are some of the signs in your community and in the world that point toward the needs in God's creation?
- Make a list of the gifts and abilities God has given you.
- Reflect and write about how your gifts and abilities intersect with the needs of the community and the world.
- List the specialized ministries that would be required to respond to the needs.

The Pastoral Ministry of the Elder

In The United Methodist Church, a pastoral charge consists of one or more local churches or congregations to which an ordained minister or local pastor is appointed as pastor in charge. Additional ordained ministers or local pastors may be appointed to larger churches as associates. In some instances, two pastors may be appointed as copastors to a parish. Sometimes several local churches may form a cooperative parish, group ministry, or extended parish that has a staff including more than one ordained minister and other paid staff persons. The paid church staff of larger churches or cooperative parishes may include administrators, educators, music and age-group specialists, and others who provide services to congregation and community. Some of these persons may be diaconal ministers; others may be mission personnel of the General Board of Global Ministries.

Whether the parish is large or small, the tasks of the ordained minister who is a pastor are similar. Consider, for a moment, the duties of a pastor as outlined in the following reflection.

Reflection: The duties of a pastor

The pastor(s) shall oversee the total ministry of the local church in its nurturing ministries and in fulfilling its mission of witness and service in the world by: (1) giving pastoral support, guidance, and training to the lay leadership in the church, equipping them to fulfill the ministry to which they are sent as servants under the Lordship of Christ; (2) providing ministry within the congregation and to the world; (3) ensuring faithful transmission of the Christian faith; (4) administering the temporal affairs of the congregation.

— *¶331, 1996 Discipline*

In the context of these basic responsibilities, a pastor gives attention to four basic areas of duty:

1. Preaching, Teaching, Worship
- preaching and teaching the word
- overseeing the worship life of the congregation
- administering the sacraments
- overseeing the total educational program of the church
- leading the congregation in evangelistic outreach
- instructing candidates for church membership

2. Pastoral Care
- counseling those struggling with personal, ethical, or spiritual issues
- visiting in the homes of church and community
- participating in community and ecumenical concerns
- searching out men and women for Christian vocations
- giving leadership for discipleship in the world

3. Equipping and Supervising
- ordering the life of the congregation
- offering counsel and theological reflection
- selecting, training, and deploying lay leadership
- participating in denominational and ecumenical programs
- assuming supervisory responsibilities within the connection

4. Administration
- being the administrative officer
- being responsible for goal setting and planning
- administering the provisions of the *Discipline*
- giving an account of pastoral ministries

Pastors vary widely in their interests, skills, and attitudes. These characteristics, combined with the needs of the parish, lead pastors to devote quite different proportions of time to the major tasks of the pastor described above. Though the pastors of large churches may specialize in one or two of these basic areas of responsibility, most pastors must attend to all of the duties while, at the same time, caring for their own personal needs and the needs of their families. The following reflection will give you insight into the ways in which these duties are lived out in a variety of settings.

Reflection: A journal of pastoral ministries
Sunday: **John is a recent seminary graduate appointed as an associate pastor of a large suburban church. He was up earlier than usual this morning because it was one of the few Sundays of the year that he would preach at the 8:30 a.m. and 11:00 a.m. worship services. Normally his participation in worship is confined to the reading of scripture or a prayer. Though preaching, he still gave leadership to a young adult class at 9:45 a.m. and met with the youth at 7:00 p.m. in the evening. At the end of this busy day, Tim wanted to discuss how to help a friend on drugs. John spent the afternoon with his family.**

Monday: **Doug and Sandy are a clergy couple assigned to a rural circuit. After breakfast they went to work on the worship plans for the coming Sunday and reviewed their busy schedule for the week. While Sandy read some background material for her sermon, Doug prepared a column for the church newsletter. Their work together was cut short when Sue Gibson came by to ask Doug for help in finding a convalescent home for her 86 year-old mother. After lunch, Sandy visited several members in the hospital while Doug contacted the director of a United Methodist home to find out what options were open to Mrs. Gibson. After supper, Doug met with his Council on Ministries while Sandy relaxed after a busy day.**

Tuesday: **Rod is the pastor of a growing urban African-American congregation. At 6:30 a.m. he was out of the parsonage sitting on the bench at the bus stop talking with people as they left for work. By discovering who they were and what they did, he had an opportunity to do some street counseling and introduce them to the ministry of the church. By 8:00 a.m. he was at the hospital with the Jacksons during Mr. Jackson's surgery. The family had a lot of questions about hospital procedures, death, and faith. This was his first opportunity to become better acquainted with this family. He returned to the church office about 10:30 a.m. and completed plans for the Sunday service. Rod had lunch with a committee working on ways to get tutoring services for children who are not sufficiently served by the existing public school programs. Later in the day he saw a man who needed help getting a job, a couple that is getting a divorce, and a teenager who thinks she is pregnant.**

Wednesday: **Juanita is a local pastor of a small Hispanic congregation trying to establish itself in a satellite city of a major metropolitan area. The Spanish population of the city**

has grown rapidly as migrant workers, immigrants, and transient families settled into this relatively small urban area. About 10:00 a.m. Juanita met with the personnel manager of a local factory to see if there were any jobs open for the unemployed of her community. A few jobs, menial in nature and paying minimum wages, were there. In the afternoon she walked through the neighborhood talking with the people she saw and uncovered more needs than she could ever hope to address. She was joined by her lay leader at 7:00 p.m., and together they sat down with the board of trustees of the church which allows them to share facilities. There is frustration over the additional maintenance costs of housing two congregations in the same building. Juanita yearns for the day when her congregation can have a church building of its own.

Thursday: **Linda is the pastor of a small-town church. After getting her youngest child off to school, she headed for a meeting with the other pastors of the district. They discussed special offerings and plans for a lay leadership training program and then were addressed by an interdenominational panel of clergy on the ecumenical concerns of the district. During lunch, Linda received word that Mr. Young had died and the funeral would be on Saturday afternoon. She left the luncheon early and went directly to the Young residence. Sandra Young and the children were upset and needed Linda's support and prayers. She stayed with them the rest of the afternoon. After supper with her family at 6:00 p.m., she met with the team of visitors who would go to visit in the homes of new residents, visitors to the church, and the sick or bereaved. Their awareness of Mr. Young's death made them more sensitive to the importance of their tasks.**

Friday: **George is a pastor in a cooperative parish ministry. He began this morning as he has most Friday mornings, completing his preparations for the Sunday service. His review of the service was cut short, however, with the arrival of other members of the parish leadership team. They spent the next several hours evaluating their work in the parish, sharing mutual concerns, and discussing how to do a better job with persons facing crises. Their meeting concluded with lunch. George enjoys the support he gets from other members of the leadership team. He can't imagine effective parish ministry without it. George did some running in the afternoon and spent the entire evening with his family. Though he received several phone calls around dinner, he scheduled appointments for the week to come with those who wished to see him.**

Saturday: **Paul is a Korean pastor who is working hard to develop a small congregation in a metropolitan area. He was up** early, as usual, and began the day in prayer with his family. They prayed for one another, the church, the needs of its members, and the world. Another busy Saturday had begun. After breakfast Paul read a little, reworked a section of his sermon and made copies of the Sunday bulletin. He then spent a few hours calling on church members before returning to the church for an afternoon youth meeting. Soon after the youth left the church, a young couple arrived with their friends and family to rehearse a wedding which would take place on Sunday afternoon. After a rehearsal dinner, Paul had time to spend with his preschooler before he put her to bed. Paul and his wife have adapted to their work schedules by looking to the middle of the week for the family time they often miss on weekends.

Chaplaincy and Extension Ministries

One of the ways ordained clergy serve God and extend the ministry of the church is through "appointments to extension ministries of elders in full connection under endorsement by the General Board of Higher Education and Ministry and other ministry settings which the bishop and conference board of ordained ministry may designate. The board shall annually verify the appropriate employment of persons under its endorsement and request their reappointment."(¶335.1.b, *1996 Discipline*)

Persons serving in these unique settings are expected to have specialized training to qualify for endorsement. A primary difference between these appointments and the local church is the nature of the institutions in which ministry takes place and the role of the minister in relationship to those settings. Ordained ministers appointed to these extension ministries serve in institutions whose primary purposes are education, international security, peacekeeping, incarceration, hospitalization, or profit. Though the purposes and environments differ from the local church, this does not mean that those endorsed have ministries which are in any way less valid than the ministries of the local church. They too are servants of God ministering to the deepest needs of humanity. Their ministries are as profoundly representative of the ministry of God through Christ as the ministries expressed through the local church.

Military Chaplains

War is inimical to the teachings of Jesus, but the role of a military chaplain is not to justify war. A chaplain's task is to minister to the emotional and spiritual needs of service members in war and in peace.

The chaplain serves units that not only prepare for war but a number of other deployments as well. The military services are involved in peacemaking, peacekeeping, and humanitarian operations both domestic and international.

Counseling takes place on flight lines, in motor pools, aboard ships, and in field positions. In addition worship services are conducted in beautifully appointed chapels on military posts and bases in the United States and overseas. Programs of religious education and youth ministry are provided for the service member and his/her family.

Hospital Chaplains

Every day hospital chaplains help patients and their relatives cope with sickness, disability, and even death. In mental hospitals, the problems are perhaps even more excruciating in some ways. Chaplains in these settings are part of a team. They work shoulder to shoulder with doctors, nurses, psychiatrists, and social workers.

The role of the chaplain is to provide pastoral care for patients' families and for staff. They reach out to persons on the wards and in the surgery and critical care waiting rooms. Frequently they will be on ethics commit-

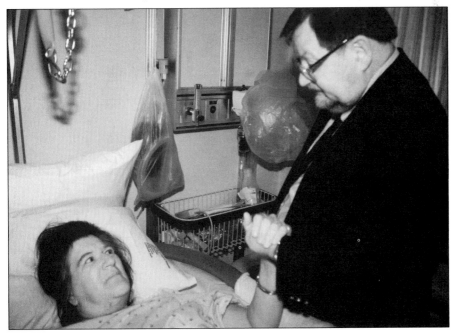

tees as they deal with complex issues of modern medicine. They frequently lead Bible studies and conduct worship services in hospital chapels.

Industrial Chaplains

The success of industry is measured by the rate of production and flow of profit. The industrial chaplain stands in the middle of the needs of management and the men and women who power the industrial machine. When these people arrive on the job, they bring with them everything that is going on in their lives —from the joy of a firstborn baby to a nagging problem with alcohol —and inevitably it affects their job performance.

Chaplains provide a ministry to people in business and industry, responding to individual and family needs as well as work-life concerns such as job stress and career. They provide a preventative as well as a problem-solving ministry that reaches out with a concern for all people.

Chaplains work with industrial management at a number of levels. They frequently train supervisors on the line to relate more effectively to their people who appear to be suffering from a personal problem. The chaplain is also influential at the policy level, conferring with management when new policies are proposed. Individual counseling frequently leads to referrals to in-house programs or community social services.

Prison Chaplains

"I was in prison and you visited me. . . ." (Matthew 25:36) In the correctional setting (prisons, jails, detention facilities), chaplains have the opportunity to be pastors to unique and diverse communities, in both traditional and nontraditional ways. They preach, teach, baptize, serve Holy Communion, counsel, visit, and serve the prisoner congregation. They are pastors not only to inmates but also to the staff and the families of both communities. They serve and are available to all the people incarcerated in their institution, providing for the spiritual needs of persons regardless of their religious affiliation. This involves recruiting, training, supervising a broad variety of religious volunteers from surrounding communities. They serve as a link between the religious communities on the outside and the religious communities on the inside, helping to build bridges of care and service both ways.

Pastoral Counselors

All pastors counsel persons, but pastoral counselors endorsed by the Section of Chaplains and Related Ministries have undergone additional specialized training so they can bring together resources of scripture and faith and the insights of the behavioral sciences. Pastoral counselors serve on the staff of a local church, in a pastoral counseling center, or in a health care institution. They work with individuals, families, and groups where their counseling is carried out within the tradition, beliefs, and resources of the faith community.

The Uniqueness of Ministry Endorsed by the Section of Chaplains and Related Ministries

Clergy endorsed by the Section of Chaplains and Related Ministries operate in pluralistic settings. They serve people who may or may not be United Methodists. In fact, many may be agnostic, indifferent, or even antagonistic to a religious faith. Yet strangely, there is identification with the minister if the minister is credible and relevant to the needs of the individual within that institution. A person lying in a hospital bed may say, "This is my pastor," and develop a close relationship because of the intimacy of crisis.

This ministry usually takes place in ecumenical settings. Involved clergypersons tend to share a common core of professional responsibility. They nurture the total religious community, encourage moral responsibility, and provide a climate for growth and maturation regardless of creed. As clergypersons of different faiths work together, they may recognize their common goals and develop objectives that can be accomplished together. They may operate from the same offices, share the same worship facilities and support staff, and coordinate their work schedules.

Endorsed clergy know that they not only serve people as individuals or groups but also serve their institutions. They must be aware of the way decisions about policies are made and participate in their formulation to ensure that structures do not dehumanize people within their institutions. Therefore, they are regular participants in the meetings which are chaired by the director or commander of their institution. They provide input, staff papers, and make recommendations as advocates of the people they serve.

Endorsed clergy are concerned about the general welfare of all the people with whom they serve. They are humanitarians in the best sense of that word. Most of their ministry takes place outside the chapel walls. They tend to meet people in the crises of their lives — where they live, walk, and move — rather than through structural contacts as clients coming to them in the context of their office or chapel.

These ministers operate in a mobile environment. In most cases the people whom they serve are transient. Their ministry, therefore, is not to a stable congregation but to a rapidly passing parade.

Endorsed clergy may conduct programs which are not denominational in focus but which may be characterized as human growth or character building programs. They may lead in educational programs which do not prepare persons for church membership but which, in all actuality, prepare people to lead more congruent, ethical, and moral lives.

Reflection
- Do you sense a call to a particular extension ministry of the church?
- What specific gifts, training, education, work experiences of grace do you bring to the unique requirement of this specialized ministry?
- Can you work collegially with ministers of other religious bodies to provide for pastoral care of all persons?

Ministry in Higher Education

The United Methodist Church supports more than 700 persons who serve as ministers in higher education. Some of these are campus ministers working in Wesley Foundations (United Methodist campus ministry units). Other campus ministers work in ecumenical units, cooperating in the name of United Methodism with one or more other denominations. Still others are chaplains at United Methodist-related colleges and universities. Some are ordained; others are not. Some work full time on campus; others hold part-time positions.

For all of them, ministry in higher education varies in response to the characteristics of the campuses they serve. It is one thing to develop ministry programs in the environment of a residential campus where students spend 24 hours a day, but quite another challenge to work in the setting of a large, urban, commuter campus where students spend little time on the campus before or after classes. While ministry with students is the central emphasis of campus ministry in The United Methodist Church, campus ministers are concerned also with faculty, staff, and administrators. As the name implies, campus ministry is a ministry to the whole campus.

Ministry in higher education is also 200 people gathered for a weekend conference to examine sexuality from sociological, psychological, and theological perspectives. It could mean a lively discussion about religion and the arts, or about religion and the anatomy lab.

The concerns of campus ministers and chaplains range from pastoral care and counseling of faculty, staff, and students, to providing a place for fellowship and spiritual nurture, to calling people to deal with social justice issues from a faith perspective.

The people with whom campus ministers and chaplains work range from 18-year-old high school graduates to 55-year-old faculty members. They may be ethnic minority students and staff; second-career and returning women undergraduates; medical, science, and law school graduate students.

In addition to caring for people and calling for them to grow in faith, ministers in higher education also care for the institutions of learning in which they serve. They raise issues about values and education, about what it means to be an educated person and a Christian, and about the role of education in our society.

Campus ministry is financed by annual conferences and local churches in cooperation with the college or university involved, by ecumenical groups in which the campus ministry participates, or by the college or university itself. Campus ministers who are ordained elders and deacons in full connection are not only employed by a college, university, or ecumenical agency but are also appointed by the bishop of the annual conference.

At independent, church-related colleges and universities, the chaplain may be part of the student affairs area or the department of religion. Church-related institutions usually provide on-campus space for the chaplain's office and activities.

At public colleges and universities, the campus ministry often is located adjacent to the campus in a church-owned building, although some schools may provide space on the campus itself for offices and/or activities. Campus ministries at some public colleges, especially commuter and community colleges, may not be based in an office or a building at all. Many of these campus ministers work out of local churches or offices in their homes, and do much of their ministry within the context of the community college's own cycle of activities. Some campus ministers and chaplains teach courses in religion and other disciplines; some teach courses for credit in the curriculum, while others teach noncredit courses. Campus ministers and chaplains who teach for credit often have completed, in addition to their theological degree, a doctorate (Ph.D., Ed.D., Th.D.) in the academic area they teach.

In addition to campus ministers and chaplains, many ordained elders, deacons, and diaconal ministers teach in university departments of religion, while others teach in departments such as philosophy, psychology, sociology, English, economics, and other areas. As a college or university teacher, the individual is employed as a faculty member, thus meeting the same academic preparation requirements as other faculty, in addition to those required for the ordained or diaconal ministry. The annual conference may appoint an ordained minister to this employment, provided the university already has accepted her/him as a faculty member. Some ordained elders, deacons, and diaconal faculty, in addition, may enter administrative positions in the college or university, such as counselor, dean, or president.

Mission Personnel

God calls all persons to be in mission. The United Methodist Church seeks to offer a variety of ways in which United Methodists can make an appropriate response.

The General Board of Global Ministries (GBGM) "is a missional instrument of The United Methodist Church, its annual conferences, missionary conferences, and local congregations in the context of a global setting." (¶1301, *1996 Discipline*)

It is the responsibility of the General Board of Global Ministries:

1. *To discern those places where the gospel has not been heard or heeded and to witness to its meaning throughout the world, inviting all persons to newness of life in Jesus Christ through a program of global ministries.*

2. *To encourage and support the development of leadership in mission for both the Church and society.*

3. *To challenge all United Methodists with the New Testament imperative to proclaim the gospel to the ends of the earth, expressing the mission of the Church; and to recruit, send, and receive missionaries, enabling them to dedicate all or a portion of their lives in service across racial, cultural, national, and political boundaries.*

—¶1302, *1996 Discipline*

"After that, the Lord commissioned seventy other disciples, sending them in front of him two by two to every town and place that he intended to visit himself."

—Luke 10:1 (translation by James Moffatt)

Commisioned Personnel
Missionaries

The 1988 General Conference provided for the commissioning of persons into a single category of mission service by the General Board of Global Ministries. These persons are assigned according to their gifts, graces, talents, and abilities; and to the need for personal involvement in meeting the goals of mission today.

Missionaries serve in many different capacities to enable the church's mission. They may serve as teachers in mission schools and on college campuses, giving guidance to students struggling to discover who they are.

They are serving on the staffs of church-related social welfare agencies as executive directors, program directors, outreach workers, and community organizers. They serve troubled women and children and people who may be hungry, homeless, underemployed, or jobless. They serve the urban and rural poor as well as those of special need. Through their witness and ministry they symbolize the church as a caring community.

Missionaries serving beyond the U.S. carry out mission strategies within the context of the cultural and historical understandings out of which relationships have developed with Christian communities in these nations. Missionaries are commissioned for service within Central Conferences, affiliated autonomous churches, autonomous Methodist Churches, United Churches, and other ecumenical bodies.

Church and community ministry enlists and trains lay leadership. Their workers demonstrate concern for human rights and the welfare of all persons. They seek to help clarify needs, assist churches and communities in developing strategies and programs, and advocate for justice. They serve in cooperative parishes, districts, annual conferences, and regional and national projects. The average term of service is six to eight years. As local leadership emerges these workers move on to new assignments.

Those persons previously commissioned to the office of home missionary, and who choose to continue in that office, are so recognized.

All the provisions that pertain to the office of deaconess also pertain to those continuing in the office of home missionary.

Deaconesses

The *office of deaconess* was established in the Methodist Episcopal Church by the General Conference of 1888. Deaconnesses are women who have been led by the Holy Spirit to devote their lives to Christian service under the authority of the church. The purpose of the program is to express representatively the love and concern of the faith community for those in need, and to enable, through education and personal involvement, the mission and ministry of the church. Deaconesses may serve any agency or program of The United Methodist Church, and in other agencies or programs pending approval by the General Board of Global Ministries and the bishop of the receiving area. (¶1313, *1996 Discipline*)

Mission Interns

The *Mission Intern Program* is a young adult mission program of the GBGM. Mission interns participate in an extensive three-year program of service during which 16 months are spend outside the United States, followed by an additional 16 months served within the United States.

Mission interns engage in mission through faith, action, education, and advocacy in response to challenges within the Third World to change systemic attitudes and structures adversely affecting the quality of human life. The program is a model of Christian mission involvement, intentionally developing global community.

US-2s

The *US-2 Program* is a young adult mission program of the General Board of Global Ministries. US-2s participate in a two-year leadership development program in the United States. Assignments for these young adults relate to mission institutions and projects, with emphases on community development and ministries of health and welfare. Settings include community centers, urban ministries, shelters for battered women, and schools. The program helps young adults to explore church-related vocations.

National Plan for Hispanic Ministries

The *National Plan for Hispanic Ministries* assists annual conferences in organizing ministries specifically related to Hispanic populations. NPHM missionaries are selected in partnership with the conferences and are strategically assigned to assist in congregational development and community organizing.

Noncommissioned Personnel
Summer Interns

The *Summer Intern Program* is a short-term mission opportunity specifically for college students. Summer interns spend 10 weeks during the summer serving in agencies related to the General Board of Global Ministries. The program provides young adults with an introduction to mission in the United States, while enabling them to gain experience related to their vocational goals.

Lay Missioners

Lay missioners are noncommissioned persons whose missional intent is to fulfill specific tasks in home mission projects. They give evidence of commitment to Christian mission and have the skills, training, and experience required for the position to be filled, as determined by the program agency. To qualify for this designation lay missioners are employed from beyond the geographical area and are contracted for service with the local project according to guidelines of the General Board of Global Ministries.

Community Developers

The 1968 General Conference authorized the *Community Developers Program*. Funded by the Human Relations Day Offering, this program is an example of what faith in God can accomplish. The program is operated from a local church base, thereby nurturing the community and strengthening the church. Community developers are selected by the local church, and they serve in consultation with the General Board of Global Ministries.

The two basic components of this program are Black Community Developers (BCD) and Indigenous Community Developers (ICD). The latter includes Hispanics, Asians, and Native Americans. Community developers are a means by which the church becomes an instrument for liberating God's people.

Mission Volunteers

Mission volunteers are lay and clergy persons who donate their time and services for a certain period of time. They may serve in teams or individually. In principle, volunteers can do any type of work or activity in which a church or church institution, agency, or project is involved, upon request by host agency. Carpentry, painting, plumbing, teaching, financial planning, and health care are a few of the examples of the types of projects undertaken across the global church.

While *Americorps*, *Medical Fellowships*, and *Disaster Response Teams* reflect the diversity of volunteerism, the *Volunteers In Mission Program* is the largest volunteer movement in the church. Most annual conferences—and each of the jurisdictions—have designated a VIM coordinator, who works cooperatively with the General Board of Global Ministries for the general coordination of this ministry.

Heads of Agencies

Persons serving as the executive directors and administrators of GBGM-related institutions are also recognized as national mission workers. They are selected by the board of directors of community centers, schools, colleges, residences, and childcare facilities, where they are employed in consultation with the General Board of Global Ministries.

Chapter 3

Steps into Servant Leadership

Leadership and the Ministry of the Laity

. . . Christian ministry is the expression of the mind and mission of Christ by a community of Christians that demonstrates a common life of gratitude and devotion, witness and service, celebration and discipleship. All Christians are called to this ministry of servant-hood in the world to the glory of God and for human fulfillment.

. . . The outreach of such ministries knows no limits. Beyond the diverse forms of ministry is this ultimate concern: that all persons will be brought into a saving relationship with God through Jesus Christ and may be renewed after the image of their creator (Colossians 3:10). This means that all Christians are called to minister wherever Christ would have them serve and witness in deeds and words that heal and free. . . . This ministry of all Christians in Christ's name and spirit is both a gift and a task. The gift is God's unmerited grace; the task is unstinting service . . . Entrance into and acceptance of ministry begin in a local church, but the impulse to minister always moves one beyond the congregation toward the whole human community. God's gifts are richly diverse for a variety of services; yet all have dignity and worth.

—¶¶104-106, *1996 Discipline*

You know you're being called, but to what? You feel compelled to respond, but you aren't sure how. Too often the first thought is to seek out ordained ministry when you are probably being called to serve right where you are. Remember that we are all called to be in ministry. You have been fortunate to have recognized it. But, now what?

There are some things you can do to get your bearings. You can test yourself. Learn your spiritual gifts. Ask yourself what you enjoy doing. What satisfies you? What are you good at? The answers should help you. You might get involved with Lay Speaking Ministry which can be very helpful in getting you in touch with your call. Most of all, pray. Pray persistently for guidance, and it will come. Jesus admonishes us to be persistent and expectant in the words "Ask, and it will be given you; search, and you will find; knock, and the door will be opened for you." (Matthew 7:7).

Whatever ministry or ministries you find you are called to, there is one thing that will certainly be asked of you, and that is servant leadership. This is a term often voiced by the church but little understood or practiced. It is a lot of things, among them listener, servant, follower, and partner, in addition to leader. The secular world has caught on to the desirability of this type of leadership because it works, it doesn't make enemies, and it obviates most of those things about leaders that other people don't like. Jesus is the ultimate model of the servant leader, but certainly not the only one. While we all doubt that we can live up to the standard he set, virtually every skill he exhibited can be learned. Some quotes from Jesus that will give you illustrations of the servant leader are Matthew 9:35-38, Luke 22:24-27, and John 13:3-5. See also, Isaiah 42:1-6 and Jeremiah 23:5-6. Once you get the idea, you can find many more examples. Robert Greenleaf, founder of the Greenleaf Center for Servant Leadership, describes the servant leader this way:

> *It begins with the natural feeling that one wants to serve, to serve* first. *Then conscious choice brings one to aspire to lead. . . . The difference manifests itself in the care taken by the servant—first to make sure that other people's highest priority needs are being served. The best test, and difficult to administer, is: Do those served grow as persons? Do they,* while being served, *become healthier, wiser, freer, more autonomous, more likely to become servants? And, what is the effect on the least privileged in society; will they benefit, or at least not be further deprived?**

Learn all you can about servant leadership. It is another touchstone in helping you with your call.

The opportunities for ministry as a layperson are all around you, wherever you are. Let's look at some of them:

• Leadership in your local congregation—there are many areas in which capable lay leadership is critical. In the church of the future it will be even more important as the threatened shortage of pastoral leadership materializes. Lay leaders are the partners of pastoral leaders. Teaching, assisting in worship, and seeing to the upkeep and business affairs are areas where we can be involved in real ministry.

• Community service—here's where the opportunities become endless. Some of these will center within your congregation; most will not. Charitable service agencies cannot live without volunteers to perform functions that range from running the agency to performing physical labor. Many need expert help with systems and methods. You can easily find out about needs simply by calling the agencies or United Way. Remember that involvement in scouting and Little League also fall into this category.

• Political activism — town boards, school boards, and leading or being

part of efforts to effect change can be great opportunities. Gambling is an issue that has been successfully countered by activists in many areas. Civil rights for minorities would never have gotten anywhere without organized activism. There are always good causes that need support.

- Your job — some professions are natural fits with ministry because they deal directly with helping people. Police, physicians, attorneys, psychologists, and teachers are just a few examples. Many others provide opportunities to minister to people, though perhaps not quite as directly. Remember that you can always be a witness to what you are, whatever your vocation is.

- In the employ of the church—local churches, annual conferences, and general church agencies do employ laypersons for a variety of functions. Program people, maintenance people, business managers, clerical staff, and professional musicians are jobs frequently filled by laypersons in local churches. Church agencies also use professional and clerical laypersons for a variety of jobs.

- At home, at school, at play — this is a reminder that you can be in ministry anywhere. In fact, if you are tuned in to witnessing and serving, you will see opportunities as they present themselves. Family is an extremely important opportunity for you, especially as it relates to the responsible rearing of children.

- Keep tuned in — your call may change. You might even be called to change positions or professions. Look at your call closely because you can always bloom where you've been planted.

Reflection

You are being called. What do you do next? Here are a few suggestions.

- Learn your spiritual gifts. Find out what you have to offer in service to your Lord. There are a number of good vehicles for doing this available from Cokesbury, especially the *Ministry Inquiry Process* guidebook.
- Write a résumé. This will help you to take inventory of your experiences, training, preferences, and education. It will make you think about what you'd like to do.
- Talk it over with your pastor and with others whose objectivity you trust. If you are married, you must include your spouse. Simply talking about what's happening to you will bring enlightenment.
- Increase your activity level in your local church. Get into things. This will provide some of your answers.
- If you can do it, get into a Disciple Bible Study group or some other serious Bible study for knowledge and spiritual depth.
- Pray persistently for direction. Watch and listen carefully for answers that *will* come. You will be given direction.
- Take the Lay Speaking Ministry Basic Course. This will help you discern your call.

---

*Robert Greenleaf, *Servant Leadership*, (New York: Paulist Press, 1977), 13.

Steps into Ordained Ministry

Ordained ministers are called by God to a lifetime of servant leader-ship in specialized ministries among the people of God. Ordained ministers are called to interpret to the Church the needs, concerns, and hopes of the world, and the promise of God for creation. Within these specialized ministries, deacons are called to ministries of Word and Service, and elders are called to ministries of Word, Service, Sacrament, and Order.

—¶116, *1996 Discipline*

Candidacy for ordained ministry is the first set of formal steps through which a person moves toward annual conference membership and ordina-tion as a deacon or an elder in full connection.

STEP 1: The Inquiring Candidate

- The journey into ordained ministry begins with participation in the *Ministry Inquiry Process*. To begin this journey a candidate should read *The Christian as Minister* and work through the *Ministry Inquiry Process* guidebook with a guide trained for this task by the district Committee on Ordained Ministry, or conference Board of Ordained

Ministry (¶306.1, *1996 Discipline*). Copies of *The Christian as Minister* and the *Ministry Inquiry Process* may be purchased from Cokesbury.

- If after completing the *Ministry Inquiry Process*, the inquiring candidate wishes to explore the call to ordained ministry, she/he may write to the district superintendent, be assigned a mentor, and enroll in candidacy studies through the General Board of Higher Education and Ministry.

STEP 2: The Exploring Candidate

- The exploring candidate shall apply to the district superintendent in writing for admission to candidacy studies. The person shall have been a member in good standing of the same local United Methodist

congregation for at least two years, including a year of service in some form of congregational leadership.

- The candidate is assigned to a mentor by the district Committee on Ordained Ministry (dCOM) or the district superintendent as its agent. The candidate is also given an enrollment form which shall be signed by the district superintendent and the mentor.
- The candidate enrolls in the candidacy studies by sending the enrollment form and the score sheet from the *Inventory of Religious Activities and Interests* (IRAI) to the Division of Ordained Ministry, General Board of Higher Education and Ministry, P.O. Box 871, Nashville, Tennessee 37202, along with a check or money order for $50. The $50 fee includes the cost of the *Candidacy Guidebook*, the *Inventory of Religious Activities and Interests*, the scoring of psychological assessment instruments where required by the Board of Ordained Ministry, and general administrative expense.
- The candidacy mentor helps the exploring candidate examine the call of God in light of the biblical record, the role and function of United Methodist clergy, personal gifts and grace, and evidence of leadership. Utilizing new or confirmed insights that are specific to ministry and highlighted in this process, after completing the first two chapters of the *Candidacy Guidebook*, the candidate then makes a commitment to the form of ministry felt to be most appropriate. (¶306.2, *1996 Discipline*).

STEP 3: The Declared Candidate

- Persons seeking to become certified candidates for ordained ministry shall consult with the pastor and Pastor/Staff Parish Relations Committee after formulating a written statement reflecting on their call to ordained ministry and requesting recommendation for certification.
- The committee shall interview each candidate and make a report to the charge conference.
- After two public announcements have been made, the charge conference votes to recommend (or not to recommend) the candidate to the district Committee on Ordained Ministry. To be valid such a recommendation must be confirmed by a two-thirds majority vote. In addition, the candidate shall have been graduated from an accredited high school or received a certificate of equivalency. (¶306.3, *1996 Discipline*)

STEP 4: The Certified Candidate

- The candidate appears before the district Committee on Ordained Ministry for examination and completes psychological assessment as required by the annual conference.

- The candidate submits a written response to questions found in the *1996 Discipline* (¶306.4) regarding God's call to ordained ministry; one's personal beliefs, gifts, and usefulness as a United Methodist minister; and evidence of understanding the ministry of the deacon and elder in The United Methodist Church.
- The candidate agrees to maintain the highest ideals of Christian life as set forth in the *1996 Discipline* (¶¶64-70).
- The district committee votes to confirm the person as a candidate and may offer a certificate of candidacy.

STEP 5: Candidacy Renewal
- The progress of candidates must be reviewed and candidacy renewed annually by the district Committee on Ordained Ministry on recommendation of the charge conference.
- A candidate who is enrolled as a student in a school, college, university, or school of theology shall present an official transcript from the school to the district committee annually. The school shall be recognized by the University Senate of The United Methodist Church.

STEP 6: Local Pastor Studies (optional)
- A certified candidate may apply for license as a local pastor after completing studies prescribed by the General Board of Higher Education and Ministry administered by the annual conference Board of Ordained Ministry or after completing one-third of the work for a master of divinity degree.
- Licensing studies are a prerequisite to appointment as a full-time, part-time, or student local pastor.
- Local pastors must make satisfactory progress in the Course of Study for Ordained Ministry, prescribed by the General Board of Higher Education and Ministry.

STEP 7: Probationary Membership and Commissioning
- A person is eligible for election to probationary membership and commissioning in the annual conference after meeting the following qualifications.
- Candidacy requirement: Each candidate shall have been a certified candidate for at least two (2) years and no more than twelve (12) years.
- Service requirement: Each candidate shall have a minimum of two (2) years in a service setting as determined by the district Committee on Ordained Ministry. With adequate supervision, this required service may be concurrent with academic study.

- Undergraduate requirement: A candidate for probationary member-ship and commissioning shall have completed a bachelor's degree from a college or university recognized by the University Senate. Exceptions may be made, in consultation with the General Board of Higher Education and Ministry, in some instances for missional purposes for persons who have a minimum of sixty (60) hours of bachelor of arts credit.
- Graduate requirements: A candidate shall have a) received a master of divinity degree from a school approved by the University Senate, or b) received a master's degree from an approved graduate theological school, or c) received a master's degree in the area of specialized ministry in which the candidate will serve, *and* d) completed a minimum of 24 semester hours of graduate theological studies in the Christian faith (¶315.4).
- Alternate route for deacon candidate: A candidate pursuing ordination as a deacon who a) has reached 35 years of age, b) has completed a bachelor's degree, c) has received professional certification or license in an area of specialized ministry, and d) has completed a minimum of eight semester hours of graduate credit in the area of specialization and 24 semester hours of basic graduate theological studies of the Christian faith (¶315.5), may fulfill the academic requirements for probationary membership and commissioning to an area of specialized ministry.
- Local pastor's route: A local pastor who a) has reached 40 years of age, b) has completed the five year Course of Study, and c) has acquired 32 semester hours of graduate theological study or its equivalent as determined by the General Board of Higher Education and Ministry including a minimum of 24 semester hours of basic graduate theolog-ical studies of the Christian faith may fulfill the requirements for probationary membership and commissioning.

STEP 8: Full Membership and Ordination as a Deacon or an Elder

- Candidates who have been probationary members for at least three years may be admitted into membership in full connection in an annual conference and be ordained either as a deacon or an elder.
- Candidates for the order of deacon a) shall have served under epis-copal appointment in a ministry of service the entire probationary period, b) shall have been supervised throughout their probationary period by a district superintendent and a mentor assigned by the Board of Ordained Ministry, and c) responded to an examination administered by the Board of Ordained Ministry on the covenantal

relationship of the applicant to God, to the church, and to the order of deacon, as well as the understanding of *diaconia*, servant leadership, and the interrelatedness of the church and the world (¶321).

- Candidates for the order of elder a) shall have served under episcopal appointment for at least three full annual conference years while on probation, b) shall have been supervised throughout their probationary period by a district superintendent and a mentor assigned by the Board of Ordained Ministry, c) shall have satisfied the board regarding physical, mental, and emotional health, d) shall have prepared a sermon on a passage specified by the board and presented a plan for teaching a book of the Bible, and e) shall have responded to an examination administered by the Board of Ordained Ministry in the areas of theology and vocation (¶326).

For further information write:
Division of Ordained Ministry
General Board of Higher Education and Ministry
The United Methodist Church
P.O. Box 871
Nashville, Tennessee 37202-0871

Steps into Endorsement

All persons have the right to receive the full ministry of the gospel of Jesus Christ. The Church is aware of its responsibility to provide adequate professional ministry to persons in special situations beyond the local church, which calls for an ecumenical ministry to persons of different denominations and faith groups. In order to assure high standards of competence and keep faith with ecumenical agreements concerning uniform standards for ministry in special-ized settings, the Section of Chaplains and Related Ministries shall have responsibility for appointments in extension ministries. . . .

—¶1411.1, 1996 Discipline

The United Methodist Church is a connectional system. The General Conference determines which parts of that system have responsibility for various functions. Individuals are accountable to the annual conference, but standards and criteria for ordination, certification, and endorsement are established by the total church. Consequently, clergy who minister in military, industrial, health care, or prison settings are accountable to the annual conference, but they are endorsed by the Division of Ordained Ministry, Section of Chaplains and Related Ministries (SCRM) of the General Board of Higher Education and Ministry. Endorsement is the process established by the church to ensure appropriate representatives in such settings.

Who Needs Endorsement?

The *Discipline* states that SCRM has responsibility ". . . for clergy in such appointments beyond the local church (¶335) as federal and other governmental chaplaincies, health care ministry settings including pastoral counseling, industrial and community service ministries, and other related ministry settings which conference Boards of Ordained Ministry and bishops may designate."(¶1411, *1996 Discipline*)

What is Ecclesiastical Endorsement?

Ecclesiastical endorsement is an affirmation that a person is or will be performing a valid extension ministry consistent with the covenantal community of The United Methodist Church and has presented evidence of having the special education, experience, and skills necessary to perform that ministry. Endorsement is given to a specific setting. Should an individual move from one setting to another, the endorsement will be reviewed and, if approved, issued to the new setting.

Requirements for Ecclesiastical Endorsement
Basic Requirements

Persons seeking ecclesiastical endorsement through SCRM to a specific setting must meet the following criteria:

1. Ordination and full membership in an annual conference
2. Graduation from an accredited college and seminary (*Additional requirements are specified by setting below.*)

Civilian Chaplaincy (institution, industry, pastoral counseling)

Standards for endorsement include certification by the appropriate national professional certifying agency. Those recognized by SCRM include:

- College of Chaplains of the American Protestant Hospital Association (COC)
- Association of Mental Health Clergy (AMHC)
- Association for Clinical Pastoral Education (ACPE)
- American Correctional Chaplains Association (ACCA)
- American Association of Pastoral Counselors (AAPC)
- American Association for Mental Retardation/Religious Division (AAMR/RD)
- American Association for Marriage and Family Therapy (AAMFT)
- International Conference of Police Chaplains (ICPC)

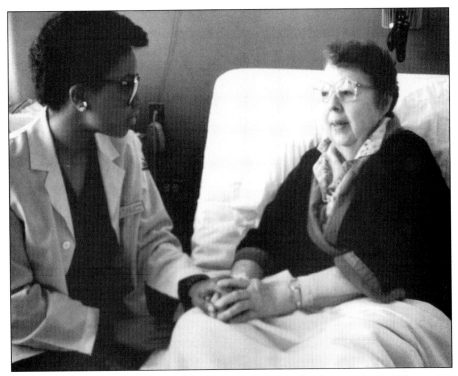

- National Institute of Business & Industrial Chaplaincy (NIBIC)
- National Association of Veterans Affairs Chaplains (NAVAC)

In situations not covered by recognized certifying agencies, SCRM will set minimum standards which will include specialized training for the type of ministry for which endorsement is sought and will include at least one year of supervised clinical training or comparable professional experience.

Military Chaplaincy (U.S. Army, U.S. Navy, U.S. Air Force)

Applicants are responsible for contacting the office of the Chief of Chaplains of the military branch for which they are seeking endorsement. The appointment procedure varies with the branch of service.

Basic requirements for initial appointment (active duty or reserve) are:

1. One must be a citizen of the United States or be a green card holder.
2. One must be physically qualified for general service based on an examination by the military.
3. One must meet current age requirements as determined by the military.

Applicants for reserve or National Guard appointment participate in the same endorsing procedures as those for active duty, and it is understood that such applicants are willing to enter active duty if called during an emergency situation. Each denomination has a quota for chaplains on active duty.

The Endorsement Process
Application

Applications are available by contacting SCRM. Specify the setting to which you want to be endorsed. Complete and return the application and required materials.

SCRM will contact your references, including your bishop and your district superintendent.

When all your materials have been received and you meet the requirements, you will be scheduled for an interview with a committee in your region. SCRM will cover your expenses for the initial interview.

The Interview

Standing interviewing committees serve each region. These committees are made up to represent the setting for which you seek endorsement.

The purpose of this interview is to understand your perception of Christian faith as related to the setting in which you desire to minister. Areas examined will include your ability to articulate a coherent theory of Christian ministry, understand and evaluate your present ministry situation, show the capacity to relate appropriately to colleagues in ministry, and demonstrate a realistic understanding of church structure and other areas which affect your ministry.

One member of the committee will serve as presenter for you and will be especially familiar with your materials.

Following the interview the committee will make a recommendation to the endorsing committee. You will be informed of the recommendation at the time of your interview, and you will also receive a copy of the written recommendation.

The committee may recommend endorsement, no endorsement, or provisional endorsement. A recommendation for provisional endorsement will include specific requirements to be fulfilled before full endorsement can be issued. Provisional endorsement is normally for a one-year period.

If you disagree with the recommendation of the interviewing committee, you may appeal the recommendation to the endorsing committee either in person or in writing. (You must, however, bear the expense for such an appearance.) **NOTE:** This process—from application to endorsement—normally takes four to six months.

The Endorsing Committee

The endorsing committee is selected from board members of SCRM and is chaired by a bishop. They meet four times a year and have responsibility for policy and practice regarding endorsement. The committee acts on the recommendation of the interviewing committee and, if so determined, will grant endorsement.

If you are endorsed, a copy of your endorsement will be sent to your employer, your bishop, and your Board of Ordained Ministry. You will receive two copies for your files.

Steps into Mission Service

Within the General Board of Global Ministries (GBGM), the *Mission Personnel Program* area serves the church in the identification, recruitment, selection, preparation, training, commissioning, care, nurture, wellness, and support of persons in mission service. For information related to mission service throughout the global church, write to:

Mission Personnel
General Board of Global Ministries
Room 320
475 Riverside Drive
New York, NY 10115
Telephone: 212/870-3660
Fax: 212/870-3774

Candidates for mission service participate in a period of preparation and training under the auspices of the *Mission Resource Center*. The center is a cooperative effort of the General Board of Global Ministries, the Interdenominational Theological Center (ITC), and the Candler School of Theology at Emory University. A program of *Missionary Wellness* is also located at the MRC in Atlanta, Georgia.

Guidelines for Selection of Candidates for Mission Service

In identifying guidelines for the selection and processing of applicants for mission service, the overall statement of the work of the General Board of Global Ministries is part of the context. Paragraph 1312 of the *1996 Discipline* states the responsibilities of GBGM. Section 6 covers the responsibilities of *mission personnel*:

a) *To promote the opportunities for mission service related to the General Board of Global Ministries throughout the constituencies of the Church.*

b) *To recruit, select, prepare and assign mission personnel, including, but not limited to, missionaries, deaconesses, US-2s, mission interns, and church and community workers.*

c) *To provide all mission personnel with preparation and training for effective service in mission.*

d) *To evaluate mission personnel for appropriate placement.*

e) *To recommend persons as candidates for commissioning as deaconesses and missionaries, and to supervise and confirm the completion of all requirements for commissioning.*

f) *To engage in supervision and support of mission personnel through referral, transfer procedures, career counseling, missionary wellness, and personnel development, assisting them in the fulfillment of their missional vocation.*

g) *To administer a diverse program of remuneration and benefits for personnel service.*

h) *To offer training for mission service throughout the global church.*

i) *To work with ecumenical agencies in fulfilling mission personnel responsibilities.*

j) *To facilitate the receiving and assigning of missionaries — lay and clergy — from central conferences and from autonomous, affiliated autonomous, and united churches, in cooperation with other boards and agencies and with annual conferences.*

—¶1312.6, *1996 Discipline*

Criteria for Selection

Four areas are covered in the selection process:

1. Christian Experience and Understanding of Mission Involvement
    The applicant shows clear evidence of Christian commitment:
    a. faith expressed personally and corporately in light of a biblical understanding of history in response to the present;
    b. active participation in a local church or worshiping Christian community;
    c. understanding of, or willingness to learn about, The United Methodist Church, its official *Discipline*, the Social Principles, the General Board of Global Ministries, and the church's connectional and ecumenical nature;
    d. awareness of social justice issues;
    e. involvement in community life and global issues;
    f. openness to various expressions of the Christian faith and to understanding of persons of other faiths.
2. Intercultural, Ethnic, and Racial Experience and Understanding
    The person's experience, background, and training indicate cultural understanding and sensitivity. Attributes include:
    a. demonstrated commitment to racial and ethnic inclusiveness in personal life and in church and society, and to the elimination of injustice;
    b. openness and sensitivity to ethnic and cultural values and practices and to racial reconciliation with justice;

c. ability to participate in and to accept the self-determination and empowerment of people;

d. awareness of and ablility to deal with the destructive nature of paternalism in mission;

e. potential for language learning and communication in a different culture.

3. Personal Relationships and Interpersonal Skills

The applicant has well developed interpersonal skills and demonstrates compassion and flexibility:

a. relates to authority in an effective way;

b. is able to form healthy and supportive relationships;

c. has personal practices commensurate with expectations for effective mission service;

d. has a strong and creative family life, where applicable, and an appreciation of mission service on behalf of all members;

e. understands sexism, racism, and classism and is committed to equal opportunity.

4. Professional Competence and Educational Preparation

The person demonstrates competence in a field of work:

a. ability to integrate professional life and Christian faith;

b. competence in a field of work through academic preparation, certification or licensing, or through life experience;

c. adaptability to different standards and practices;

d. openness to continuing education, personal development, and evaluation.

Commissioning

Commissioning recognizes, first and foremost, that persons are called by God to participate in God's mission. This calling is grounded in an understanding of Christian baptism as the call to every Christian to mission and ministry. Commissioning recognizes a vocational call to a missional task under the *Discipline* of The United Methodist Church. Commissioning signifies that the person has satisfactorily completed the application, selection requirements as determined by the General Board of Global Ministries, and a process of preparation and training for missionary service. Commissioning is a covenant among God, the individual, and the household of faith.

Such commissioning signifies covenant on the part of the deaconess or missionary to:

• proclaim Christ to the world while striving for God's reign of grace, peace, and justice;

- continue to grow and understand God's missional activities through the global, ecumenical, and interreligious community;
- interpret mission activity as practiced by The United Methodist Church through the General Board of Global Ministries;
- cooperate with the ecumenical community;
- be supportive of denominational and board policy, practice, structure, and linkages; and accept a simple lifestyle in which one may not necessarily receive benefits and/or reimbursement according to secular standards.

This covenant also signifies that for those who have been commissioned, the General Board of Global Ministries will:

- undergird them with prayer;
- actively seek mission assignments;
- provide appropriate preparation and training; and
- provide financial, spiritual, and caring support.

Who Shall Be Commissioned?

Persons who meet the following criteria for missionary or deaconess:

- Christian commitment and understanding of mission involvement;
- intercultural/ethnic/racial experience and understanding;
- personal and interpersonal relationship and leadership development skills;
- appropriate education and professional qualifications;
- physical and emotional health; and
- willingness to enter into the covenant with The United Methodist Church through the General Board of Global Ministries and commit to serving three or more years.

Steps into Certification in Areas of Specialized Ministry

The certification of educators, youth workers, musicians, and evangelists by The United Methodist Church resulted from a desire of persons in these fields to serve the church with excellence. It is available to qualifying persons whether they are lay persons, ordained deacons or elders, or diaconal ministers.

Certification is the church's recognition that an individual has met the required standards for academic training, experience, and continuing study necessary to achieve and maintain professional excellence in areas of specialized ministry.

The church's need for individuals who can serve to the best of their ability makes certification by The United Methodist Church increasingly important.

STEP 1

Persons seeking certification by The United Methodist Church in Christian education, youth ministry, music ministry, or evangelism should make their interest known to the registrar of the Division of Deacons of their annual conference Board of Ordained Ministry. For the name and address of the registrar contact your annual conference office.

STEP 2

Applicants should study leaflets HE4010 (educators), HE4040 (youth workers), HE4020 (musicians), HE4030 (evangelists), and must meet the minimum personal, church, academic, and professional qualifications listed in steps 3-6. They must be interviewed by the conference Board of Ordained Ministry to determine if they have met these standards.

STEP 3: Personal Requirements
- Recognized Christian character, personal competence, integrity, and commitment to the church's total ministry and mission.
- Ability to function with emotional maturity and sound judgement; ability to relate to people and to work with volunteers and staff.
- Demonstrated leadership; ability to integrate theory and practice; understanding of the commitment to the educational ministry of the church.

STEP 4: Church Requirements
- A full member (not an associate member) of The United Methodist Church for at least one year.

- Knowledge of The United Methodist Church's structure, polity, curriculum resources, program, and mission.

STEP 5: Academic Requirements

Applicants must meet the educational standards set by the Division of Ordained Ministry, Section of Deacons and Diaconal Ministries, General Board of Higher Education and Ministry, The United Methodist Church. There are three kinds of certification: (1) associate, (2) director, and (3) minister in each field—evangelism, music ministry, Christian education, and youth ministry. Each has its own academic requirements. It is important to carefully study the appropriate leaflet (*See STEP 2*).

For information on dates and locations of certification courses for associates currently being offered, ask the conference board for the latest listing, published annually by the Division of Ordained Ministry, Section of Deacons and Diaconal Ministries (SDDM).

To be eligible for financial assistance from SDDM, applicants must obtain an enrollment form (HE4064) for certification studies from the Division of Deacons of the conference Board of Ordained Ministry and complete the form prior to registering with the school for the first course. **NOTE:** Certification courses are not the same as the foundational studies required for diaconal ministry.

STEP 6: Professional Requirements

Persons seeking certification as directors or ministers of evangelism, music ministry, Christian education, or youth ministry must have two years' experience in the area of their respective discipline. This experience can be gained through two years in a full-time job/appointment with The United Methodist Church.

Persons seeking certification as associates in evangelism, music ministry, Christian education, or youth ministry must have four years of employment experience in evangelism, music ministry, Christian education, or youth ministry in The United Methodist Church. These four years of employment experience shall be concurrent with or may follow the certification studies but shall not precede certification studies.

STEP 7

Following the required experience for the certification being sought, individuals may apply for certification using forms HE4011 (Christian education), HE4032 (youth ministry), HE4021 (music ministry), or HE4031 (evangelism). Applicants can obtain these forms from their annual conference Board of Ordained Ministry. Applicants must send a copy of the completed application form to the annual conference Board of Ordained Ministry and a second copy to the Division of Ordained Ministry, Section of Deacons and Diaconal Ministries, P.O. Box 871, Nashville, TN 37202-0871.

STEP 8

Each applicant must submit a minimum of five references from persons acquainted with his/her personal, church, and professional qualifications.

Among the five persons must be a United Methodist minister (ordained elder or ordained deacon), a college or seminary professor under whom the individual has studied, and a general officer in a local church with whom the educator, evangelist, youth worker, or musician has worked.

STEP 9

Upon vote by the conference Board of Ordained Ministry indicating the applicant has satisfactorily met all requirements for certification, the conference board notifies the Division of Ordained Ministry that the application is approved. After satisfactory review by the division, the certificate is issued and sent to the conference Board of Ordained Ministry.

STEP 10

The conference Board of Ordained Ministry presents the certificate to the individual, possibly at a session of the annual conference.

STEP 11

Certification is subject to annual review and approval by the conference Board of Ordained Ministry. The individual must continue to meet the standards maintained by the Division of Ordained Ministry, Section of Deacons and Diaconal Ministries. Each year the conference board will send all certified persons a copy of form HE4004 which must be completed and returned by the date specified. Certification is renewable for as long as the certified person desires it, contingent upon satisfactory completion of the annual renewal form which includes an active program of continuing education and approval of the conference BOM.

Chapter 4
Guidelines for the Minister

Guidelines for the Minister

As a pastor, chaplain, campus minister, diaconal, or ordained minister of The United Methodist Church, one of the most significant and satisfying tasks you have is to help identify, advise, and assist those called to servant leadership in our denomination. The *Discipline* states that it is your duty:

> To search out from among the membership and constituency men and women for pastoral ministry and other church-related occupations; to help them interpret the meaning of the call of God; to advise and assist when they commit themselves thereto; to counsel with them concerning the course of their preparation; and to keep a careful record of such decisions.
>
> —¶331.1.p, 1996 Discipline

For many this responsibility is not so much a duty as it is the joy and satisfaction of relating to people and their deepest level of need at the time of a major vocational decision.

As a minister, you can assist those persons exploring vocational options in many ways. You can direct them to *The Christian as Minister,* a vocational guide for service opportunities in The United Methodist Church. You can meet with them and use *The Christian as Minister* and the *Ministry Inquiry Process* guidebook as the basis of a series of conversations on the meaning of Christian vocation. You can help them see beyond the seemingly impersonal, formal requirements for ministry in The United Methodist Church to the intention of the church to find the most effective persons for its leadership. You may also have opportunities to help inquiring persons examine a variety of leadership possibilities, receive feedback on their leadership potential, and test their leadership skills. You may also have insights about their family and background that will be helpful to the individuals or to the committees that may consider them for ministerial service. If you know of serious factors that may mean the individual should not be encouraged further in the exploration of a particular form of ministry, it is very important that you discuss these with the individual. Regardless of the outcome of the inquiry, you are still the individual's minister and as such, your concern is equally for the inquirer and the future leadership needs of the church.

The Christian as Minister and the *Ministry Inquiry Process* guidebook were written to assist you in your vocational guidance work with your church or constituency. In using this resource, the following guidelines may be helpful:

1. Carefully read through *The Christian as Minister* and the *Ministry Inquiry Process* and participate in any candidacy guide training offered through the district committee or conference Board of Ordained Ministry.

   • As you become familiar with their contents, you will see various ways they can be used in the interpretation of God's call to ministry. You may also discover new information about the options for ministerial service, their standards and requirements.

   • The more thoroughly you know the contents of this vocational guide, the better equipped you will be to inform your church or constituency and counsel those who sense a call to some other form of Christian service.

2. Order a supply of *The Christian as Minister* and the *Ministry Inquiry Process* for your study, church library, office, or workplace.

   • Use sections of *The Christian as Minister* with your Pastor/Staff Parish Relations Committee, confirmation class, or any other group that wishes to study the meaning of Christian vocation.

   • Give a copy to persons you believe are considering a church-related occcupation. Ask them to study the book carefully and note any questions or insight gained.

3. Offer to counsel with those inquiring into church-related occupations.
    -   Use *The Christian as Minister* and the *Ministry Inquiry Process* as resources for that guidance.
    -   Explore the meaning of God's ministry, Christ's call to servant leadership, an understanding of vocation, and the options for ministry in The United Methodist Church.
    -   Help the inquirers to see themselves as others see them and to appreciate the gifts and grace they bring to various vocational choices.
    -   Give them exposure to a variety of forms of ministry through research, observations, and interviewing.
    -   Help them to view a variety of options before making any commitments to further exploration.
    -   Once a tentative decision is made, clarify the steps to be taken in order to make that vocational choice a reality.

4. Use *The Christian as Minister* as a study guide with the Pastor/Staff Parish Relations Committee.
    -   Help the committee to gain insight into a theology of ministry.
    -   Review the committee's responsibility for interviewing and recommending candidates for ordained and diaconal ministry to the charge conference.
    -   Clarify the steps a candidate must take in order to enter ordained ministry.
    -   Discuss the resources the church can provide to assist a person who wishes to enter a church-related occupation.
    -   Identify other resources available through the district, conference, or general agencies of the church that can assist as well.

5. Maintain confidentiality.
    -   Those inquiring into church-related occupations need the freedom to explore their vocational options without a premature disclosure of their intentions.
    -   Confidentiality is needed to prevent a premature commitment of a congregation to a candidate. When this occurs, there is always the danger that an inquirer may respond by making a commitment to the wrong vocational choice or perhaps the right choice for the wrong reasons.
    -   Confidentiality at the inquiring stage is also essential for those contemplating a career change. Unnecessary pressure is often brought to bear on an employee when it is discovered that she/he is even thinking about changing careers.

Chapter 5

Guidelines for the Pastor/Staff Parish Relations Committee

Guidelines for the Pastor/Staff Parish Relations Committee

The enlistment, guidance, and support of candidates for ordained and diaconal ministry in The United Methodist Church is not a responsibility of the pastor alone. It is a duty which is shared with the Pastor/Staff Parish Relations Committee (P/SPRC). The duties of the committee include the following:

> *To enlist, interview, evaluate, review, and recommend annually to the charge conference lay preachers and persons for candidacy for ordained ministry (see ¶¶ 249.8 and 305), and to enlist and refer to the General Board of Global Ministries persons for candidacy for missionary service, recognizing that The United Methodist Church affirms the biblical and theological support of women and men of all races and ethnic origin for these ministries. Neither the pastor nor any member of the committee on pastor-parish relations shall be present during the consideration of a candidacy application or renewal for a member of their immediate family. The committee*

shall provide to the charge conference a list of students from the charge who are preparing for ordained ministry, diaconal ministry, and/or missionary service, and shall maintain contact with these students, supplying the charge conference with a progress report on each student.

—¶262.2f(7), 1996 Discipline

For the sake of the candidates and the enhancement of ministry in The United Methodist Church, this responsibility of the P/SPRC must not be taken lightly. Candidates need the affirmation and support of the committee in order to enter candidacy for ordained or diaconal ministry. They need the resources a P/SPRC can coordinate in the local church for those it recommends. Candidates will also benefit from regular contact with the committee as they prepare to meet the educational and other requirements of their vocational choice.

The P/SPRC plays an important role in the selection of qualified candidates for ministerial leadership in The United Methodist Church. No one knows the candidate better than the membership of the local church. The recommendation of the committee to the charge conference and, in turn, the recommendation of the charge conference to the district Committee on Ordained Ministry is a crucial gate through which all candidates must pass in order to enter diaconal or ordained ministry. It is the one place where the *Discipline* requires the approval of the lay leadership of the local church in the candidacy selection process. It is the one opportunity the local church has to be sure that candidates for ministry meet the criteria and expectations of the local church. If you are concerned about the quality of ministerial leadership in our denomination today, here is the place to address that need.

Finally, let it be noted that although the *Discipline* requires that only candidates for ordained ministry be enlisted, guided, and supported through the P/SPRC, there is no reason why this committee cannot involve itself in the enlistment of persons for all forms of Christian service. If the committee, the pastor, and the Administrative Board/Council so determine, the committee can have a significant impact on the way the local church looks at the matter of Christian vocation and the quality of persons enlisted for all forms of church-related service. Such a task that is done well not only affirms those persons identified as potential servant leaders, but broadens the vision of the congregation in terms of the nature of Christian vocation. It also awakens the church to the potential that exists for addressing the ministerial needs of the church and gives the local church the satisfaction of knowing that it is playing a significant role in the shaping of ministry for the future.

As you go about the work of fulfilling this responsibility in your church, the following guidelines may be helpful:

- Review *The Christian as Minister* with your pastor, and, if necessary, clarify the role of the committee in the enlistment of candidates for ministry.
- Have the chairperson of the P/SPRC meet with a candidate prior to the meeting where she/he will be interviewed to clarify the purpose of the meeting and the expectations of the committee.
- If a written statement is to be prepared, agree on the form it will take and communicate that information to the candidate.
- The meeting with the candidate may be informal and spontaneous. If the candidate is invited to make a brief oral statement of his/her current decisions and interests, the committee members and the candidate may then be free to discuss any issues that seem important.
- While conducting an interview, the committee may wish to keep in mind the historic questions first asked by John Wesley in 1746. These questions which apply to ordination as a deacon or an elder are as follows:

Wesley's Questions for Examiners

In order that The United Methodist Church may be assured that those persons who present themselves as candidates for ministry are truly called of God to this office, let those who consider recommending such persons for candidacy as ordained ministers in The United Methodist Church prayerfully and earnestly ask themselves these questions:

1. *Do they know God as a pardoning God? Have they the love of God abiding in them? Do they desire nothing but God? Are they holy in all manner of conversation?*

2. *Have they gifts, as well as evidence of God's grace, for the work? Have they a clear, sound understanding; a right judgment in the things of God; a just conception of salvation by faith? Do they speak justly, readily, clearly?*

3. *Have they fruit? Have any been truly convinced of sin and converted to God, and are believers edified by their service?*

As long as these marks occur in them, we believe they are called of God to serve. These we receive as sufficient proof that they are moved by the Holy Spirit.

—¶305, *1996 Discipline*

The decision of the P/SPRC should be based on more than just the individual's appearance and presentation to the committee. It should also consider how well this person has done in the life of the local church over an extended period of time. This is the reason for the requirement of the candidate having been a member of the local church for at least one year.

As the committee interviews a candidate for ministry, the following questions may be important:

1. In what ways has this person actually experienced God's forgiveness and grace? Does this show in the way she/he lives? How?
2. Does this person have personal habits that enhance his/her witness as a Christian? Which personal habits diminish or negate that witness?
3. What gifts, skills, abilities does this person have? Can she/he speak clearly and comfortably before a large group and in a small discussion group? What impression or feeling do you get from being with this person? Does this person seem confident, poised, relaxed, open, warm, friendly, attractive as a person?
4. How does this person relate to his/her family? Are relatives (parents, siblings, spouse if any) supportive of the person's candidacy for ministry? Is this person being discouraged by some family members? Why? Do some family members seem to be pushing this person into some form of ministry as a career? In what ways?
5. Does this person seem to have the intellectual ability (appropriate to his/her age) to study effectively and work easily with the Bible, theological issues, and the subject matter of the intended career? Has this person had relatively good grades in high school and college (if any)?
6. How does this person relate to authority persons, such as church leaders, pastors, managers, teachers, employers, and others who supervise his/her work in some way? Is this person independent, assertive, yet cooperative and pleasant?
7. What evidence of effectiveness in church-related leadership has this person already shown? Describe these. To what extent were these the result of this person's initiative and abilities, as compared to being someone else's work that this person merely followed or used?
8. What other evidence of future potential has this person shown?
9. How committed does this person seem to be to the gospel of Christ and servant ministry in The United Methodist Church? To what extent may salary, prestige, and other rewards be important to this person? How does she/he respond to discouragement, failure, disagreements, and other adverse conditions that are often part of ministry? Will this person be comfortable with the possible restrictions that ministry in the connectional structure of Methodism may impose in some situations?

10. What other evidence do you have that the person will enhance and improve the quality of ministry in The United Methodist Church?

- Before a candidate is recommended to the charge conference, the chairperson and pastor can encourage the committee members, if they have not already done so, to invite informal, confidential comments from church members and others who know the applicant. If concerns should be expressed about the applicant's fitness for ordained or diaconal ministry, the P/SPRC may want to delay making a recommendation to the charge conference until it has time to examine the comments and consult with the applicant about them.

- When announcements are made that the charge conference will be voting on a recommendation of candidacy for ordination as a deacon or an elder, an open invitation should be given to any person who wishes to consult privately and confidentially with the pastor or P/SPRC chairperson about the applicant. In this way it is more likely that varied points of view will be heard and any negative comments will be dealt with in a constructive way.

- If potential problem areas do appear from any of these sources, the pastor and the P/SPRC chairperson can decide how to use them in the most constructive manner with the applicant. It may be appropriate to consult with the person offering negative information, delay making a recommendation to the charge conference, or take other action prior to the conference if it is likely that the conference may not be able to handle the issues in a public meeting.

- If the announcements of the meeting are made properly and if no serious issues become known that should be handled privately with the applicant, the charge conference meeting provides the public occasion when the church gives its formal endorsement of the applicant.

The chairperson of the P/SPRC will want to review and emphasize the important decision facing the charge conference. Quoting from some of the *Disciplinary* statements or from the questions suggested for the P/SPRC may help the members present to see the great importance and the challenge of ordained or diaconal ministry.

- The chairperson may then offer the candidate the opportunity to make a brief presentation to the conference as a way of introducing or renewing acquaintance with all persons present.

- The chairperson of the P/SPRC should then report on the committee's recommendation to the charge conference, and the reasons for that recommendation should be spelled out in some detail.

- Time may then be allowed for others to comment and present evidence that would support or deny the recommendation.
- The general tone and atmosphere of the conference meeting should be warm, relaxed, and flexible to allow for serious consideration of the decision.
- The charge conference, like the P/SPRC must keep in mind these two objectives in its decision:
  1. To do what is in the best interest of The United Methodist Church and the enhancement of its ministry.
  2. To exhibit a pastoral concern for the individual, regardless of the outcome of the decision.
- The P/SPRC must consider ways in which it can maintain its relationship with the candidates it affirms. Candidates for ordained ministry require an annual recommendation from the committee and the charge conference until they become local pastors or probationary members of the annual conference.
- For further guidance in the work of the P/SPRC with candidates for ministry, consult the *Guidelines for Leading Your Congregation 1997-2000: Caring for Pastors and Staff*, available from Cokesbury.

If you feel led to participate in the Ministry Inquiry Process, contact the district superintendent and ask to be assigned a guide who will assist you in this open process to discern your call. The *Ministry Inquiry Process* guidebook can be obtained directly from Cokesbury.

Appendix

United Methodist Schools of Theology

Boston University School of Theology
745 Commonwealth Avenue
Boston, MA 02215

Candler School of Theology, Emory University
202 Bishops Hall
Atlanta, GA 30322

Claremont School of Theology
1325 North College Avenue
Claremont, CA 91711-3199

Drew University, The Theological School
36 Madison Avenue
Madison, NJ 07940

Duke University, The Divinity School
107 New Divinity, Box 90968
Durham, NC 27708-0968

Gammon Theological Seminary
P.O. Box 92426
653 Beckwith Street, SW
Atlanta, GA 30314

Garrett-Evangelical Theological Seminary
2121 Sheridan Road
Evanston, IL 60201

Iliff School of Theology
2201 South University Boulevard
Denver, CO 80210-4798

Methodist Theological School in Ohio
3081 Columbus Pike
P.O. Box 1204
Delaware, OH 43015-0931

Perkins School of Theology, Southern Methodist University
Kirby Hall
Dallas, TX 75275-0133

Saint Paul School of Theology
5123 Truman Road
Kansas City, MO 64127

United Theological Seminary
1810 Harvard Boulevard
Dayton, OH 45406-4599

Wesley Theological Seminary
4500 Massachusetts Avenue, NW
Washington, DC 20016